THE MINERS OF WABANA

The Story of the
Iron Ore Miners of Bell Island

Gail Weir

Canadian Cataloguing in Publication Data
Weir, Gail, 1948-
Miners of Wabana
(Canada's Atlantic folklore and folklife series, ISSN 0708-4226 ; no. 15)
      1. Iron miners - Newfoundland - Wabana - History.
      2. Iron mines and mining - Newfoundland - Wabana - History.
      3. Wabana (Nfld.) - History. I. Title II. Series
HD8039.M72C38 1989   C89-098643-6622'.341'09718
ISBN 0-920911-69-2, ISBN 978-0-920911-69-2

Cover: Teamster Gordon Helpert with mine horse 'Max,' August 1949
Library and Archives Canada/Credit: George Hunter/National Film Board
Photothèque collection/PA-128002

Title Page: A "brass," assigned to each miner, was used to keep track of
those men working in the mines on any given shift (see pages 100-101).

Canada Council   Conseil des Arts
for the Arts   du Canada

We acknowledge the financial support of The Canada Council for the Arts
for our publishing activities.

Canadä

We acknowledge the financial support of the Government of Canada
through the Canada Book Fund for our publishing activities.

Printed in Canada.

BREAKWATER BOOKS
WWW.BREAKWATERBOOKS.COM

My father, Stanley Hussey,
who was a miner until his death in 1961,
dearly loved Wabana, a name with which he
associated the whole of Bell Island.
I dedicate this book to him and to all the
miners who worked there.

CONTENTS

Acknowledgements 7

Foreword to First Edition 9

Foreword to Second Edition 13

One: History of the Wabana Mines 21

Two: Labour History 32

Three: Tragedies in The Tickle 45

Four: The Miners 54

Five: The Working Life 85

Six: Skylarking 111

Seven: Mishaps, Ghosts and Fairies 124

Eight: Life After DOSCO 161

Appendix: The Murals Project 175

Works Cited 194

Endnotes 198

ACKNOWLEDGEMENTS

MANY PEOPLE HELPED in the research and writing of this book and I wish to thank them all for their help. First and foremost are the men and women who so willingly shared their memories so that this piece of Bell Island's history could be preserved: Eric Luffman; Harold Kitchen and his wife Una; George Picco and his wife Sarah; Albert Higgins; Ron Pumphrey; Len Gosse; Clayton Basha and his wife Lillian; an eighth miner and his wife, who wished to remain anonymous; and my mother, Jessie Hussey. My brother, Don Hussey, submitted to my questions on growing up in the home of a miner and also sent me material of interest, including some from acquaintances in Nova Scotia who had survived the ore boat sinkings in Conception Bay during World War II. My sister, Phyllis, her husband, Ken Parsons, and my sister, Bonnie, all answered many "what do you remember about" questions.

While doing the original research for the 1989 edition, the following people and organizations helped me locate the many pieces of information, documentation, student papers, statistics, photographs, slides and films related to the mining years of Bell Island: my co-workers in all divisions of the Queen Elizabeth II Library, especially the Archives and Manuscripts Division, the Centre for Newfoundland Studies and Inter-library Loans; the staff of the Memorial University of Newfoundland Folklore and Language Archive; the Provincial

Archives of Newfoundland and Labrador; MUN Maritime History Archive; MUN Anthropology Department's Archives of Undergraduate Research on Newfoundland Society and Culture; the Provincial Reference Library; the National Film Board of Canada and the Library and Archives Canada; Roger Carter of MUN Extension Services; Art King and Derek Wilton of MUN Earth Sciences Department; William Wegenast and Howard Dyer of MUN Engineering Department; Maurice Scarlett and Ches Sanger of MUN Geography Department; Norm Mercer, John Fleming and Paul Dean of the Provincial Department of Mines and Energy; and Roger Guest of MUN Physics Department.

I am grateful to Peter Narvaez of MUN Folklore Department, who supervised me during the writing of the thesis upon which this book is based, for his valuable guidance and encouragement at that time.

For this new edition of the book, I am grateful for assistance and encouragement from members of the Bell Island Heritage Society, especially Clayton King, Paul Connors of the IAS Committee, Brian Burke of the Murals Project, the Board of the Bell Island Community Food Bank, Henry Crane, the Bell Island Town Council, and the late Charlie Bown, whose enthusiasm for all things Bell Island continues to be an inspiration.

My thanks go to everyone at Breakwater Books.

My husband, Harvey, daughter, Sharada, and son, Jonathan, have been behind me all the way on this project and their constant encouragement and support have kept me going when all seemed hopeless. Thank you.

FOREWORD TO THE FIRST EDITION

IN SPITE OF having been born on Bell Island, where my father, both my grandfathers and my uncles were all miners, I grew up knowing very little about the mining life. It is true that my father came home every day covered from head to toe in red dirt and I watched my mother every night as she rigged his lunch. My brother and sisters and I looked forward to paydays with great excitement at the prospect of the loose change that would be divided among us. Those were the boom years and little did we know that we would soon observe our beloved and prosperous home town go bust.

Although I was there when the iron ore was washed out of the pit clothes, I had no idea what happened underground to make them so dirty in the first place. While I saw the lunch being prepared, I could not visualize the conditions under which it would be eaten. Paydays were a godsend, but the shiny coins gave no clue as to how hard my father had to work, or under what dangerous conditions, to get them. I knew the heartache of saying good-bye to relatives and childhood friends whose families were leaving to find work in the factories and mines of faraway Ontario. I did not stop to think that most of the people on the Island had uprooted from their traditional homes to come there to work. Some of them had even come from other mines that had closed down, so this kind of upheaval was not new to them.

Indeed, I took this lack of knowledge for granted for a long time until the day came when I asked myself just what it was I did know about mining for iron ore on Bell Island. That day came when, as a student at Memorial University of Newfoundland about to pursue the degree of Master of Arts in Folklore, I had to decide on a topic for a thesis. As fishing is the main occupation in Newfoundland and as I had not been raised in a fishing environment, I thought it would be a challenge to concentrate on some aspect of that life in order to gain some knowledge of that industry. While thinking about this idea, it suddenly occurred to me that I knew almost as little about my own father's work experience as I did about the fisherman's. I was only thirteen when he died and he had never been given to talking much about his work. As for my grandfathers, my paternal grandfather, John Hussey, had died before I was born and my maternal grandfather, John Dawe, had given up mining to run a lumberyard when I was very young as well.

This book is not about the geology of the Wabana mines. Many books and papers on that subject can be found at the Queen Elizabeth II Library of Memorial University. I was not interested so much in what the men took out of the mines as I was in what they experienced as workers in the mines, what folklorists call their "occupational folklife." I wanted to find out about their work day, the conditions they worked under in the mines, the tragedies, the mischief they got up to, the rats that depended upon them and the horses that they depended upon. I was curious to know if they were superstitious men and whether they had seen ghosts of miners who had died in the mines.

The reader should be cautioned that there are two kinds of history in this book. First there is the factual, documented history of the operations of the mining companies, the problems that beleaguered the mining unions, and the events surrounding the tragedies of the two ferries that collided in the Tickle and the torpedoing of the ore boats during World War II. Interspersed with my recording of these events are the personal experience stories of individuals who were there when these events took place or who knew of them at the time. These individuals' stories are called "oral history." As any accident investigator will tell you, it is very rare for two individuals to agree on all details surrounding an accident. In the same way, while my informants told me the way they remember certain events as having taken place, there are going to be readers who will read one or another of these accounts and say, "I was there and that's not the way it happened at all." I was not so concerned with whether or not an informant got the facts of an event straight as I was with how he or she remembered it and how it affected them at the time. Each person's story is important and helps to round out the historical picture for future generations.

The majority of the interviews for this research took place over a period of a year, from May 1984 to May 1985 and involved eight former miners. All of them began working with the mining operation as boys, the oldest starting age being eighteen and the youngest being eleven. All but one of them continued to work with the Company until the mines closed. Five miners' wives also contributed valuable information. In addition to these interviews, during the spring and summer of 1985, an archival search was undertaken for materials that related to the lives of the miners. Any material gleaned from the student papers at the Memorial University of Newfoundland Folklore and Language Archive is cited in the endnotes as being from MUNFLA. The audio tapes produced while researching this work are also housed there.

The mines had been closed for eighteen years when I began my research for this project. I was concerned that with each passing year, the miners who could tell what the early days of the mines were like were decreasing in number. This work has afforded me the opportunity to record some of their knowledge and experiences. At the same time I have gained for myself an understanding of "where I came from." I was always proud of it and, now that I know more about it, I am prouder still to be called a Bell Islander.

Gail Weir
St. John's, Newfoundland
August 29, 1989

FOREWORD TO THE SECOND EDITION

IT IS ALMOST 17 years since the first edition of *The Miners of Wabana* was published. A lot has happened on Bell Island in those 17 years, especially in the area of cultural-tourism. The population has continued the slow but steady decline that followed the large out-migration of the 1960s when the mines closed. From the 1986 Census through to the 2001 Census, there was a loss of an average of 100 people every year. In spite of this, or perhaps because of it, there has been an increasing interest in celebrating the Island's history. The first manifestation of this was in film, books, and numerous magazine and newspaper articles. In 1974, Memorial University's Extension Services produced a film about the Island's mining history entitled *Wabana*, directed by Joe Harvey. John W. Hammond published *The Beautiful Isles: A History of Bell Island from 1611-1896* in 1979 and *Wabana: A History of Bell Island from 1893-1940* in 1982. Kay Coxworthy edited three volumes of stories and reminiscences starting with *Memories of an Island* in 1985. The first edition of this book, *The Miners of Wabana*, was published in 1989. Coxworthy's second book was *Tales From Across The Tickle* in 1993. Steve Neary compiled a detailed account of Nazi U-Boat activity in Conception Bay, entitled *The Enemy On Our Doorstep* in 1994. Coxworthy's last book was *The Cross on the Rib* in 1996. These attempts to record the Island's mining history and personal experience stories were no doubt, in part at least, a response to the loss of visual clues to that history. Following the shutdown in 1966, many of the mine buildings and equipment were dismantled and removed, leaving little indication of the great industry that once prospered there. Today, one has to know where to look to see the few mine-related structures still standing. The entrance to No. 4 Mine is still intact in a meadow near the air strip. What used to be the Survey Office on No. 2 Road served for a time as the Town Hall. No. 3 Hoist House has done duty as the Town Council garage. The former Union Hall is now a warehouse. Along No. 2 Road, Bennett Street and West Mines Road, many former "Company" houses are now sporting vinyl siding and vinyl slider windows. The one-story houses are harder to spot, but the 11/2 story houses are distinguishable from privately-built houses by their high gabled roofs and attached porches.

Wabana Mines: A National Historic Site

When visitors arrive on Bell Island, they can now see tangible evidence of the Island's glorious history thanks to the efforts of volunteers working in conjunction with the Town Council. One such volunteer was Steve Neary, who had been Bell Island's government representative for many years. After much lobbying on his part, monuments were erected during the 1990s to commemorate significant events in the Island's past. First of all, the Historic Sites and Monuments Board of Canada declared Wabana Mines a National Historic Site in 1988. The Board unveiled the plaque "commemorating the national historic significance of the Wabana iron ore mines" on September 5, 1991. The ceremony took place at the commemorative site just east of the Post Office on No. 2 Road. The Seamen's Memorial Monument at Lance Cove was unveiled November 2, 1994 in memory of the 69 seamen who lost their lives in the autumn of 1942 when German U-Boats attacked ore boats that were anchored near the Island and at the pier. And, finally, the Memorial Monument to those lost in the collision of the passenger ferries *The Garland* and The *Little Golden Dawn* in the Tickle in November 1940 was unveiled at the Beach on November 10, 1995.

The Bell Island Museum and Underground Tour

Throughout the 1980s and 90s, the Bell Island Heritage Society, a small but energetic group of volunteers, worked with the local Economic Development Officer and Island Advisory Services, actively looking for ways and means to bring about positive changes in Bell Island's economic picture. As part of their tourism initiative, they worked tirelessly to establish a miners' museum on the Island. In part due to the momentum created by the high level of activity for the year-long 1995 Centennial Year Celebrations, a year of activities marking 100 years since the first shipment of iron ore left Bell Island, their hard work came to fruition with the opening of a temporary museum on No. 2 Road in July 1995. It had always been the intention of the Heritage Society to open No. 2 Mine for tours and this dream finally came true in July 1998. Of the 3000 people who went through during that first season, fewer than 10% were residents of the Island, proving that this attraction had great potential for bringing new money into the community. A new museum building was constructed above the entrance to the No. 2 Mine tour. The building opened for visitors in the summer of 2000, with the official opening taking place July 25, 2002 when Lieutenant Governor Max House cut the ribbon.

Place of First Light: The Bell Island Experience

In 1997, a young St. John's theatre producer named Anna Stassis was inspired by the miners' own personal experience stories that she read about in the 1989 edition of *The Miners of Wabana*. She and director Danielle Irvine founded First Light Productions and set about producing "Place of First Light: The Bell Island Experience," which ran throughout the summers of 1997, 1998 and 1999. This half-day travelling show wove together live theatre and sightseeing, including scenes enacted on the ferry as it crossed the Tickle and at the monuments described above. The show culminated in "the underground experience" in No. 2 Mine in which the audience played the roles of novice miners, and such historic characters as Union President Nish Jackman came to life. The entire show was based on true stories and the audience was left with a sense of the spirit and personality that characterize Bell Islanders, and the hard work, joys and sorrows experienced by the iron-ore miners. The show moved the audience between laughter and tears and brought the cultural heritage of the Island into sharp focus. It received rave reviews from the press and the audiences and was named a theatrical landmark event by the Professional Association of Canadian Theatres. Because of the prohibitive costs of mounting such a large and ambitious show, it did not continue after the 1999 season. However, when Governor General Adrienne Clarkson and her husband, author John Ralston Saul, paid a Vice-regal visit to the province in June 2000, the mine portion of the show was re-enacted at her request as she was especially interested in seeing how Bell Island was preserving the memory of its mining heritage through art.

The Murals Project

Another way in which the Island is preserving its heritage through art is in the Murals Project. No other effort has brought so much positive publicity to Bell Island. A special appendix has been added at the end of this edition of the book to relate the history of this project.

In Memoriam

Sadly, six of the people who contributed so much to this book have passed away:

Leonard Gosse died June 22, 1987
Harold Kitchen died August 1, 1993
Eric Luffman died December 30, 1993
George Picco died April 4, 1997
Sarah Picco died April 7, 2001
Albert Higgins died September 18, 2002

As I reread the book in preparation for this new edition, I could not help but remember them with great fondness and appreciation.

Gail Weir
St. John's, Newfoundland
February 28, 2006

Miners in No. 3 slope wait at the end of the shift for the man tram to take them to the surface, August 1949. Some of the men near the front are (from left to right): Pat Power, Herb Wareham, Mark Gosse, Albert Slade, Eugene Kelloway, Dick Gosse, Gordon Power, Gerald Littlejohn, Graham Deering, Ambrose Bickford, Jack Deering, Doug Noseworthy, Joey Parsons, Bert Hynes, Bill Penny, Ned Hickey, Harold Kitchen, Lewellyn Meadus, Harold Miller (sitting), Tom Galway.

"Gold is for the mistress-silver for the maid –
Copper for the craftsman cunning at his trade."
"Good!" said the Baron, sitting in his hall,
"But Iron-Cold Iron-is master of them all."

Rudyard Kipling
Cold Iron

ONE

History of the Wabana Mines

The like land is not in Newfoundland
for good earth and great hope of Irone stone.

Henry Crout

BELL ISLAND IS located in Conception Bay on the northern part of the Avalon Peninsula in Newfoundland, Canada. Its dimensions are approximately 6 miles (9.5 km) long by 2 miles (3 km) wide. The former mining district of Wabana is located on its north shore. Portugal Cove lies approximately 3 miles (5 km) by water to the east, and the capital city of St. John's is 9 miles (14.5 km) by road from Portugal Cove.

Bell Island appears in stark contrast to the surrounding shoreline of Conception Bay. At many points along its perimeter the reddish-brown cliffs drop several hundred feet straight down to the ocean. There are only a few places where the land dips gracefully to the sea. A rock that resembles an inverted bell lies off the southwestern end of the Island. Lewis Anspach reported as early as 1819 that the Island's name was derived from this resemblance.[1] Known as "Great Belle Isle" by its original inhabitants, the name "Bell Island" came into popular use around the end of the nineteenth century as the iron ore mining operation attracted people from Canada and other parts of Newfoundland.

Prior to 1895 when the mining operation began, Bell Island was sparsely populated by Irish and English settlers who farmed the rich topsoil and carried their produce in sailing vessels to St. John's and points around Conception Bay. Evidence shows, however, that iron ore was mined on Bell Island in an earlier period as Anspach wrote, again in 1819, "there is an iron-mine at Back-Cove, on the northern side of Bell-Isle." He received his information from oral sources and, unfortunately, does not elaborate on this mining operation.[2] Much earlier than this, in 1578, Anthony Parkhurst, a Bristol merchant who made four voyages to Newfoundland, reported that he had found "certain Mines...in the Island of Iron, which things might turn to our great benefit...for proof whereof I have brought home some of the ore."[3] And one of the members of John Guy's colony, Henry Crout, wrote glowingly of Bell Island saying, "the like land is not in Newfoundland for good earth and great hope of Irone stone."[4] Despite these reports, it was not the British who eventually invested in Bell Island.

On August 4, 1892, the Butler family of Topsail paid sixty dollars to file three applications for licenses to search for minerals on the north shore of Bell Island.[5] They had shown a sample of the ore to the captain of an English vessel, who said he thought it might be valuable and took a piece of it to England with him. He wrote some time later asking for "fifty pounds for analysis," but the Butlers thought it was money he wanted and did not reply. One of the younger Butlers, who went to Canada to seek his fortune, wrote back to Newfoundland and requested that a sample of the ore be sent to him. The result of this analysis was good, and the Butler group took out the three leases on the north side of the

Island. They then engaged the dry goods merchants, Shirran and Pippy of St. John's, to act as their agents in finding a developer for the property. These agents brought in the New Glasgow Coal, Iron and Railroad Company, which had begun life as the Nova Scotia Forge Company in Trenton in 1872. It was later called the Nova Scotia Steel & Coal Company (hereafter referred to as the Scotia Company) and built a steel plant near New Glasgow in 1880 at a place it christened Ferrona, where it poured the first steel ingots in Canada. Upon investigation of the Bell Island site, this Company agreed to pay the Butlers $120,000 if they decided to purchase the property, which they eventually did on March 4, 1899.

C.R. Fay wrote in 1956 of an interview he conducted with a grandson of one of the Butlers, who stated that the value of the ore on Bell Island was discovered by accident.[6] His grandfather had a coasting boat running from Port de Grave to St. John's. On one trip, when he was caught in a strong wind, he stopped at the north side of Bell Island and took on ballast. At St. John's, while unloading the ballast, he was approached by a foreign-going skipper, who offered to take a sample and have it analyzed. Some time later, after ignoring the request for the "fifty pounds for analysis," his grandfather, who had by now moved to Topsail, took a prospector to the Island. Instead of his usual fee of five dollars for ferry service, Butler received a miner's claim and was told he should keep his mouth shut. The grandson says that in the end the claim brought five thousand dollars. This may indeed have been his share as there were five partners in the Butler group. They were: Jabez Butler, John J. Butler and James Miller, all farmers of Topsail; Jabez H. Butler, an electrician of Cambridgeport, Massachusetts; and Esau Butler of Charlottetown, PEI.

R.E. Chambers, the chief ore and quarries engineer of the Scotia Company, reported that he landed on Bell Island in

1893 "in company with the Messrs. Butlers of Topsail, Newfoundland, who then owned the property, for the purpose of examining the iron ore beds there."[7] One former miner, who started with the Company in 1916 at the tender age of eleven, remembers the Chambers of New Glasgow as old Bob and young Bob, and recalls:

> They were blacksmiths in their day, but they got mixed up in real estate, and they owned the Nova Scotia Steel and Coal Company in Trenton.

He says that it was the younger Chambers who came to Bell Island looking for iron ore. In the beginning, the Scotia Company did not want people to build homes on Bell Island. They wanted them to live in Portugal Cove and area and commute to the Island, going to their homes on Saturday evenings and back to the Island to work on Monday mornings. They could not know the extent of the ore deposit and may have feared the eventual shut-down that would leave the workers and their families separated from alternative work by a body of water.

In the summer of 1895, when the mining of Bell Island iron ore was started and preparations were being made for the first shipments, Thomas Cantley, who was secretary of the Scotia Company, named the mine site "Wabana." This is an *Abnaki* Indian word which, literally translated, means "the place where daylight first appears."[8] Since the Island is by no means the most easterly point on the continent, the name does not seem quite suitable until one considers the comment made by the late Addison Bown, who compiled a newspaper history of the Island, that it is "a particularly appropriate title for the most easterly mine in North America."[9]

Just 350 miles from the Cape Breton soft coal fields, Bell Island's location was ideal for the Scotia Company. Its position

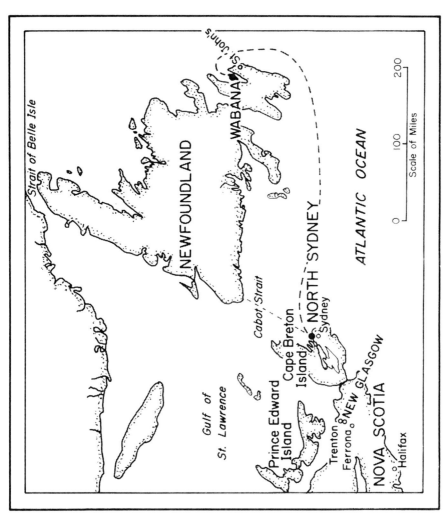

Sketch map showing Wabana
in relation to the iron and steel
works of Sydney, Nova Scotia.

in the most easterly part of the North American Continent meant that the mines were directly on the marine track of North Atlantic shipping. Cantley wrote that this was regarded as an extremely attractive feature:

> ...for perhaps the most necessary requirement for an iron property, after the quality and quantity of the ore shall have been assured, is its geographical position. Indeed, accessibility is fundamental. From Wabana, situated midway between Europe and America, the seaboard markets of both continents lie open.[10]

The first shipment of ore left Bell Island destined for Ferrona, Nova Scotia, on Christmas Day, 1895.[11] The first shipment to the United States left the Island on July 3, 1896, and on November 22, 1897, the first trans-Atlantic shipment left for Rotterdam.[12]

At the same time as the Scotia Company was starting operations at Wabana, an American industrialist, Henry Whitney, established the Dominion Coal Company to consolidate most of the coal mines in Cape Breton. He hoped to merge with the Scotia Company to build a steel mill at Sydney. When this merger failed, he led a consortium that incorporated the Dominion Iron and Steel Company (DISCO).[13]

In 1898, Sir Charles Tupper, a Canadian statesman, told the Sydney Board of Trade, "the iron ore of the Wabana mine will lead to the establishment of a steel industry in Sydney."[14] Indeed, a decade later, Chambers attributed the establishment of Canada's first fully-integrated, primary steel-producing plant at Sydney to the deposits of iron ore at Bell Island and, as he put it, this plant transformed Sydney from "little more than a village...into a bustling cosmopolitan city."[15] In fact, Bell Island and Sydney had a symbiotic relationship that lasted for the life of the Wabana mines and for most of the life of the Sydney steel mill. They were each dependent on the other and, as the fortunes of the operations in Sydney went, so went those at Wabana. The histories of each would have been very different without the other.

Originally the mining of Wabana's red haematite was a surface operation, but it was soon discovered that the main ore deposit lay under the floor of Conception Bay in a series of beds, which dip at approximately eight degrees towards the northwest. In 1899, the Whitney-led DISCO bought the lower bed from the Scotia Company, while the Scotia Company retained the upper bed in which the ore contained a higher percentage of iron. Included in the sale was a submarine area of about three square miles adjoining the shore. Following this sale, the Scotia Company bought the General Mining Association coal fields in Nova Scotia and transferred its basic steel-making operations from Ferrona to Sydney Mines, where it began constructing its steel plant in 1900 to supply its finishing mills at New Glasgow. DISCO began constructing a basic iron and steel plant in Sydney that same year. Both plants used Wabana iron ore with first steel produced at DISCO's plant by the end of 1901 and at Scotia's plant in 1902. The Sydney plant used Wabana ore as its sole source of supply of blast furnace ore until the 1950s, and its existence was the foundation stone of the Cape Breton coal industry.[16] During the two years 1912 and 1913, the Wabana mines provided almost half of the total amount of iron smelted in all Canada.

Work began on driving the slopes, or shafts, to the submarine areas at Wabana in March 1905. The Scotia holdings were reached in 1909. By 1911, the Scotia Company owned thirty-two and a half square miles of the submarine area, and DISCO owned eight and a half square miles.[18]

In April 1920, a young journalist, who would one day lead Newfoundland into Confederation with Canada, visited

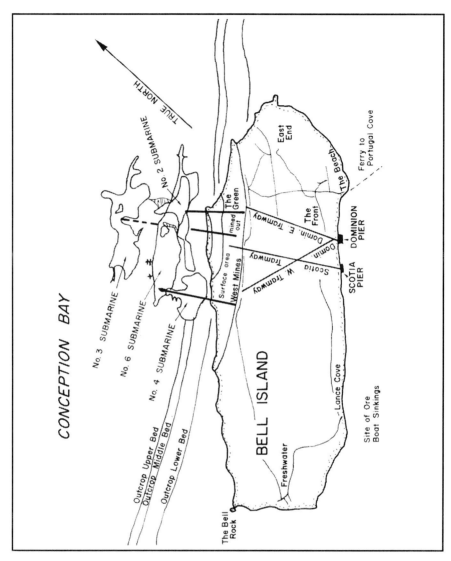

Map of Bell Island with sketches showing the position of the submarine mines in 1951. Based on a map found in C. M. Anson, "The Wabana Iron Ore Properties of the Dominion Steel and Coal Corporation, Limited." Canadian Mining and Metallurgical Bulletin 473 (1951): 597.

Bell Island for the first time to gather material for a series of articles for *The Evening Telegram*.[19] In those articles Joseph R. Smallwood described the interior of the mines and how the ore was extracted. He toured No. 2 slope, which was nearly a mile long at the time, and remarked that walking back up the fifteen-degree slope reminded him of walking up Blackhead Road, a long, steep hill in the southwest of St. John's. By 1951, ore was being mined three miles out to sea. The minimum cover for submarine mining was fixed at two hundred feet from roof to sea bottom but, as the extremities were reached, it ranged up to sixteen hundred feet.[20]

Following World War I, British industrialists looked to Canada's coal and iron companies to help renew the British economy. They enlisted Roy Wolvin, president of the Halifax Shipyards Limited who had become president of DISCO by 1919, and Dan McDougall, president of the Scotia Company, who conspired in 1920 to create Canada's largest corporate merger. They formed the British Empire Steel Corporation (BESCO) which absorbed both the DISCO and Scotia operations, including their Wabana iron ore properties, the Halifax Shipyards, and most of the Nova Scotia coal mines.[21] BESCO was soon in financial difficulty, one of the first manifestations of which was the closing of the Sydney Mines steel plant that had been operated by the Scotia Company. In 1926, BESCO went into receivership and was taken over by its mortgager, the National Trust Company. In 1930, all the assets of BESCO were bought by the Dominion Steel and Coal Corporation, known as DOSCO, the name associated with "the Company" through its subsequent title changes. DOSCO was part of a large British conglomerate. Dominion Wabana Ore Limited, a subsidiary of DOSCO, controlled the mines from 1949 until 1957, the most prosperous period in Bell Island's mining history. Then, after a fierce battle among DOSCO's major shareholders, A.V. Roe Canada Limited, which later became Hawker Sidley Canada Limited, took over.[22]

At the taking of the 1891 census, two years before the Scotia Company appeared on the scene, Bell Island had 709 residents. By the 1901 census, there were 1,320 residents listed, of which 199 were employed in mining. There seems to be a contradictory statement in this census when it is noted that 1,100 men were employed in the mining operation.[23] Actually, many of the men working on Bell Island at that time maintained their homes in communities around Conception Bay and, thus, did not list themselves as residents. Ten years later, Cantley said of the labour conditions on the Island:

> ...the working population is almost constantly on the move. This is due largely to the circumstance that for generations the fisheries have given employment to the Newfoundlander, and a relatively small class has as yet forsaken this vocation to engage in mining.[24]

In January 1950, No. 2 Mine became the first of the four mines that had been operating since the 1920s to shut-down.[25] The remaining working mines were then No. 3, No. 4 and No. 6. Even with this closure, the population continued to rise and by 1951 had reached 10,291.[26] Of these, 1,994 were employed in ore operations and 7,499 were their dependents. These people made up 95 percent of the Island's population.

A paper presented to the Canadian Institute of Mining and Metallurgy that year expressed great optimism for the future of the Wabana mines and talked of the millions of dollars worth of improvements that would be undertaken in the coming years.[27] Indeed, from 1950 to 1956, an extensive expansion and modernization program was carried out. Machines now loaded the ore that was once shovelled by hand, and electric locomotives replaced the horses that used to haul cars, while on the surface a new concentration plant removed rock that had formerly been picked out by hand. This program cost approximately twenty-two million dollars and seemed to be paying off, as it was noted in 1957 that "ore from Wabana is finding increasing acceptance in European markets."[28] By 1958, the number employed in mining had peaked at 2,280.[29] Then, in May 1959, No. 6 Mine was closed for good. Shipments from Wabana reached a zenith a year later at 2.81 million tons, and the population peaked at 12,281 a year after that. It is little wonder that residents were confused by the close-down of No. 4 Mine in January of 1962 and shocked when the closure of the final mine, No. 3, was announced on April 19, 1966.[30]

While all the expansion was going on and glowing predictions were being made, Sydney, which owed its very existence to Bell Island and had always been Wabana's best customer, had been going to Labrador and Venezuela for higher grade, non-phosphoric iron ore concentrates in order to reduce high operating costs.[31] At the same time, competition had been increasing in the international iron ore market because of a growth in the availability of high-grade ores from West Africa and South America.[32]

Wabana was Canada's oldest, continuously-operating iron mine when it ceased production on June 30, 1966 after 71 years of activity.[33] The total ore shipped between 1895 and 1966 was approximately 79 million tons. Almost half of this was used in Canada, while the remainder was exported to such countries as West Germany, Britain, the United States, Belgium and Holland.[34] Despite its closure, it has been proven that ore can still be mined in accessible areas for a further twenty years at a rate of two million tons a year.[35]

TWO

LABOUR HISTORY

We notified the Company we were going to be off and
the Company only laughed. Monday we called her off.

Len Gosse

THE SEVENTY-ONE years of the mining operation on Bell Island were not without labour problems. Low pay and a high rate of accidents caused much dissatisfaction among the workers in the early years. Wars, politics, depressions, world economies and market conditions all affected the operation of the mines, sometimes bringing boom, more often causing slow-downs or even compulsory "vacations."

On August 24, 1896, only eight months after the first shipment of ore, Bell Island had its first miners' strike. One hundred and eighty men struck for twelve cents an hour, two cents more than they were already getting. They were pacified by the promise that their grievances would be brought to the Company's attention. The raise never came through.[36] I.C. Morris, a St. John's writer, visited the Island in August 1899. While riding in an ore car, he noticed that someone had written on the side, "I am killing myself for 10c./H."[37]

In 1900, there was a second, more serious strike with 1,600 men involved, 1,100 of whom were organized into their first Union, known as the Wabana Workmen and Labourers' Union. This time the demand was for fifteen cents an hour. It was also stated by Thomas St. John, the Union president, that the strike had been precipitated when the Dominion Company had attempted to reduce the number of men hand-loading ore cars. One in every four men was to be let go, and three men were to load two cars between them, instead of the usual two men per car. When these orders came, the miners stopped work and became involved in demonstrations and parades. Violence was threatened when longshoremen were brought from St. John's to load an ore boat. All available policemen were summoned to the Island. Things calmed down when it was believed that a settlement had been reached, but soon there were more problems. St. John's police had to be called again when the Dominion Company had their office staff go to the pier to unload a schooner of coal. The resulting riot ended with the Union officials being arrested. The strike finally ended when E.M. Jackman negotiated with the companies for a settlement, which became known as the "Treaty of Kelligrews" because that was where the negotiations took place. The agreement was for twelve and a half cents an hour for skilled miners and eleven cents for ordinary labourers. The Union dissolved once the strike ended.[38]

Mining was extremely dangerous in those early days of the Wabana mines. There were so many accidents that the government passed Newfoundland's first Mining Act in 1906 to provide for inspectors to investigate practices and conditions in the mines. This "Regulation of Mines Act" was the basis for all such subsequent Acts in Newfoundland. Still, there were 74 serious mine accidents in a two-month period in 1908 caused by the introduction of a powerful new explosive.[39] In spite of these factors, the several attempts that were made to form a Union over the next few years were unsuccessful.

A group of disgruntled miners did finally manage to form another Union in 1923: The Wabana Mine Workers' Union was registered on December 4th of that year under the signature of John P. Skanes, President. A month later, Joshua Humber became its first elected president. For just over a year, this Union was affiliated with the International Union of Mine, Mill and Smelter Workers as Local 152, but it did not seem to gain any benefits from that association. Instead of negotiating directly with the Company, the Wabana Mine Workers' Union negotiated through the government.[40] This was probably because previous attempts by Humber and others to talk to Company officials had met with failure. This was not surprising as BESCO, the Company that had taken over both the Dominion and Scotia companies in 1920, was in big financial trouble. Frustrated by their inability to make any headway with BESCO, Humber and Skanes had been sent to Sydney by their fellow workmen in the fall of 1923 to see if they could enlist help from Unions there, but Humber was turned back by immigration officials in North Sydney, accused of being a labour agitator, and Skanes would not go on without him. Things came to a head in 1925 when BESCO introduced punch-clocks. Until then, the men had always gone home when they had their quota of work done, whatever time of day that was. The Union won on this issue, and the clocks were taken out. Another concession won at this time was the right to be paid in cash instead of by cheque.[41]

In 1926, the Union purchased land on Davidson Avenue and built their first Union Hall. In spite of this, interest in the Union waned to such a low level that for the next 14 years, whenever there was a grievance, instead of enlisting the help of the Union, those involved would form a workmen's committee to deal with the situation.[42] An example of this occurred on April 21, 1928 when the face cleaners in No. 3 Mine struck for higher pay, resulting in the mines closing down. At a mass meeting that afternoon in the C.L.B. Armoury, a committee was struck to send a petition for higher wages to the National Trust Company in Montreal, the mortgager that was temporarily managing the operations following the bankruptcy of BESCO. Representatives of head office arrived on Bell Island at the end of May to negotiate with the miners' committee, but refused to allow the M.H.A. for the district, Major P.J. Cashin, to sit in on the meetings because he was not an employee of the Company. When the Major raised the matter in the House of Assembly, Prime Minister Monroe replied that he did not consider it necessary to have a member of the government present as the miners' delegates had impressed him as "intelligent and reasonable men" who, he felt, were quite capable of conducting their own negotiations. A wage increase of three cents an hour for all classes of workmen along with a new bonus scale was agreed upon a few days later.[43]

It was not until 1941 that a Union with some real clout was formed by David Ignatius (Nish) Jackman. This Union was made up of five locals, each with its own executive officers.

No. 1 Local comprised all those men who worked on the surface. The four other Locals were No. 2, No. 3, No. 4 and No. 6, the numbers of the four operating mines. On the title page of the minutes book of No. 6 Local, someone wrote, "From 1923, when the Union was registered, nothing happened. This Union began to function when Nish Jackman took over in 1941."[44]

Nish Jackman was born on Bell Island in 1902 to Catherine (Malcolm) and David Joseph Jackman. Nish's father had been born in St. John's, where he apprenticed as a tinsmith. He established a smithy in the mining town of Little Bay in

1887 and relocated to Trinity East in 1890, moving back to St. John's in 1895, the same year that mining got underway at Wabana. In 1899, he moved to Bell Island to work as a tinsmith with the Dominion Company, and started his own general business in 1901. He was active in community affairs and was the first chairman of the local council formed in 1917. He later served as postmaster. Nish attended school on Bell Island and at St. Bonaventure's College in St. John's. He worked in the United States during the 1920s.[45]

Eric Luffman remembers the Jackman family:

> Nish's father was a merchant at the Front of the Island, tinsmith and a merchant. [Nish] had one sister. His brother, Frank, was a parish priest up in Topsail. They were fine people, come from a good family of people.

Jackman believed in Union ideals even when he was a boy, as demonstrated by the following story Eric tells from their childhood:

> Myself and Nish and Ches Greening used to go around picking up rubber overshoes, you see, and sell the rubbers, two cents a pound to old Nikosey, who lived [and had a shop] on Town Square. The serving girls in the big houses, you see, used to put the rubbers out on the platform, so we'd get them, too. And Nish was our treasurer. He never cheated us, not one cent, from the time we started until we broke company, and we used to go all over the Island picking up rubbers. A pair of long rubbers would bring twenty cents.

Nish was a nephew of E.M. Jackman, who had negotiated the "Treaty of Kelligrews" in 1900. E.M. Jackman had a St. John's tailoring business and was known as "Jackman the Tailor." He had been President of the Tailors' Union in the 1880s and had been instrumental in organizing other tradesmen into unions, hence his involvement in helping negotiate an agreement in the 1900 strike.[46] Nish's cousin, Walter Jackman, was also very active and served on the Wabana Mine Workers' Union executive as Vice-President. Aside from a family history of union involvement, Nish had participated in union activities in the United States.[47] Len Gosse, who had been active with the Union at Wabana, recalled:

> He was in the States connected with the Union up there for ten or fifteen years. That's what made him good. He had lots of experience he got in the States with strikes and everything else.

Apart from this experience, however, Jackman had "paid his dues" in the Wabana mines. According to Eric and Len:

> Nish Jackman had an awful lot of qualifications. Matter of fact, he was a lumberman first, Nish. He lost his leg in No. 2 Mine.

> He worked in No. 2 Mines. And he had an accident and lost his leg. That was in 1938, I believe. He was down in the mines flogging, putting trips in. He went down and went in and got his leg cut off, his foot and his leg removed.

The Company's announcement that work in the mines would be decreased to half-time was the catalyst that Jackman needed to get workers united into the new Wabana Mine Workers' Union. He became President in October of 1941 and negotiated directly with the Company.[48] When what was known simply as "the Union" was first started, not everyone joined right away. The minutes book of No. 3 Local for November 1941 noted:

> The General President [Jackman] then said that by all means we should take anyone in the Union, and that if the Company took one man and placed him on the Staff [ie. non-Union employee], we should take him off the Staff and throw him over the back of the island.[49]

Peer pressure was brought to bear in at least one instance, as it was reported at a Union meeting on January 28, 1942 that the Unionized men of No. 2 Mine had refused to work with non-Union members. The outcome was that out of six non-Union men, four joined up, one "drew his time" [ie. quit his job], and one did nothing.[50]

It was not long afterwards that Union dues started to be deducted at the Main Office. Eric recalls:

> I think all hands were pretty happy with the Union. You see, they were losing nothing, and they were gaining all the time. So Nish got that. I don't think there was any dispute about it at all. Everyone was awfully glad to join. I don't think anyone complained too much. The Union did Bell Island good, and it didn't hurt the Company. As long as they had a good person to negotiate with, you could always get a reasonable settlement. The Company didn't want to have strikes. But you couldn't go in and ask for something that they couldn't give you. Nish got a lot of things with no problem at all.

At the March 13, 1942 meeting of No. 1 Local, the motion was passed to acquire the former Church of England Academy on Bennett Street at the corner of Grammar Street for use as the Union Hall. At that same meeting, it was reported that:

> The President, Mr. Jackman, went on to speak of

Unionism and was very interesting. He also told of some of his experiences in Unions and charged all members to be on their guard against all rumours and to be true Union men and to be up to our slogan: "to go forward together."[51]

The Union became an affiliate of the Newfoundland Federation of Labour in 1944. It became Local 4121 of the United Steel Workers of America in 1948.[52] From this time onward, labour-management relations ran smoothly and there were no major strikes or disagreements. Eric says:

They were getting thirty cents an hour when Nish Jackman took over, and in about five or six years when we went into Confederation, there was only one place in Canada better paid than we was. He got a lot of concessions. I know one time he asked for twenty-four cents of a raise, and we all thought he was crazy. He got it and never lost a man hour.

Len remembered a dispute over wage increases:

I was Vice-President of No. 4 Local, Submarine Local, for a little over a year. On strike one day only, that was over wages. We notified the Company we were going to be off, and the Company only laughed. Monday we called her off. When all the boys went to work, we called her off, and that was it. We lost that day and that was all. The next day we went to work. Got five cents an hour increase.

Ron Pumphrey, who published and edited a weekly newspaper on Bell Island during the 1950s and 60s, remembers the Union leader well:

Nish Jackman was a diminutive, ferocious, little man.

A diminutive, ferocious man with big grey teeth, one of which was sparkling gold. And he was a fighter, a real fighter. I can see him now in the Union Hall, stripped down to the shirt. And he had one leg. He had an artificial leg. And he was a real leader. And he incited the men to unionize, to go on strike, to get their rights and what have you. And I remember, but I won't name the prelate, a certain priest who got up and denounced him as being a communist. But Nish Jackman had a lot of power, a lot of power. I had a reverence for him one time which had the elevation that one would have for his god. Until I got to know him and then I realized he had a foot of clay. [Ron laughs.] The other one was wooden. He was a ferocious little man, but I liked him.

Jackman's ability to make gains for the miners was legendary and, while he may have been fiery at Union meetings, he kept a cool head in his dealings with the Company. Eric sat in on at least one negotiating meeting and remembers it this way:

We had a meeting in the Main Office this morning over something that happened in the mines, the men went home for some reason or other. So we got in there and Nish listened to them, never opened his mouth for two hours, and then he settled the whole thing just like that. The Company were just like children as far as negotiating went. The Old Man, Proudfoot, said to me, "Eric," he said, "that's Nish Jackman. That's the way he's been for the past twenty years. When he comes in here," he said, "there's times he don't speak for three or four hours. But when he speaks, everybody listens. And he's always reasonable. He's always satisfied to compromise. If C.B. Archibald says, 'Nish, this can't be done,' he'll tell him why.

They'll go to work on it. Like getting delay caps to the blasters. Delay caps cost a lot of money." They were working on that so the blasters wouldn't have to go back in the smoke, you see. Nish worked on that for years. But Nish Jackman didn't go bawling and roaring and swearing. He went in and talked like a gentleman, and they treated him like a gentleman. No use in trying to bribe Nish Jackman. He knew nothing about the like of that.

All evidence indicates that Nish Jackman was not the kind of Union leader to take his men out on strike on a whim:

A strike would have spoiled everything. But Nish Jackman was too smart for that. Besides, that was too much work for Nish. He wasn't the kind of a man who was going to make work for himself. And he knew what he could do. Nish Jackman knew to what extent he could push, and he pushed that much and no more. He got what he wanted without any trouble. Nish was a good leader.

After the negotiating meeting mentioned above, Nish and Eric talked about strikes over a bottle of beer:

I said, "Nish, you've never had a strike." "No, Eric," he said, "strike never comes in my mind, because I know the men can't stand a strike, and I'm not going to put them into a strike. My job is to get everything I can from the Company in the peacefulest possible way. I never saw where I could do my men any good by putting them on strike. They're paying me a salary and that's all I got to do is try to get things. If I'm not able to get a raise of pay or get conditions without a strike, I'm no good. When I go in, I try to make things better for them. That's my job," he said. "If I put them on strike one week, it'll take them a month to get over it. If they're out a month, it'll take them a year to get over it. Chances are, some men with big families, chances are they'll be hungry. That's what they got me for," he said. And he was right. He was a good President. He had a lot of friends, an awful lot of friends.

Nish Jackman was a colourful character whose name became a household word on the Island, known by young and old alike. A good part of the colour, his drinking, was outwardly scorned by many, but may have served also to make this larger-than-life figure more endearing by showing him to be as fallible as the next man. Eric continues:

> Jackman was a funny man. He was a peculiar feller, very agreeable, and nothing bullying about him. The booze rules many a man, but he didn't do the Union no harm. He didn't do Bell Island any harm. I'll tell you, the men had a good, honest leader in Nish. Nish Jackman done an awful lot for the men.

Shortly after becoming the Union President, Nish once again followed in the footsteps of his uncle, E.M. Jackman, and became involved in provincial politics. The elder Jackman had served as Minister of Finance and Customs in the Robert Bond government from 1900 to 1909. In 1946, Nish was elected to the National Convention as the delegate for Bell Island. The Convention had been set up to find an alternative to the Commission of Government that had been ruling Newfoundland since 1934. One report on the Convention said of Nish:

> Ignatius Jackman, the fiery little president of the Bell Island Miners' Union, thought that since the Convention was an elected body it was far superior to the Commission of Government. "If any commissioner

dares to defy us," he said, "let us remove him and put another in his place."[53]

Nish advocated for stronger relations with the United States. He formed a "Union with America" party in 1947 and petitioned the British government to have union with the U.S. placed on the referendum ballot. He later supported Chesley Crosbie's Economic Union Party in joining forces with the Responsible Government League for the referenda of 1948. Following Confederation with Canada, he was elected to the House of Assembly twice, 1949 and 1951, as the Progressive Conservative member for Harbour Main-Bell Island. He lost the 1956 provincial election and a bid for a federal seat a few years later when he ran as an independent labour candidate. [54] Eric recalls:

> He never attended the House of Parliament [Assembly] only once. He was a P.C. That's what Smallwood[55] couldn't understand. "I never seen a P.C. in my life," he said, "in the Union." But Smallwood said this, "He was probably the best Union leader in the Dominion of Canada."

In the mid-fifties, the Union membership began to feel that he was neglecting them for the provincial political scene. There was also dissatisfaction with some of his policies, and some felt that his drinking interfered with the performance of his Union duties. The combination of these things led to his being ousted as Union President when the 1956 vote was taken. Ruben Rees was elected President in his place, but resigned a year later. Jackman was returned to office when elections were held the following year, and by 1963 he had gained such favour that the Union voted him a pension for life. Only a year later, however, in the June 1964 election, he was voted out of office for the last time and was replaced by his long-time rival,

John S. Power. Power was to remain President until the Union's charter was revoked in 1967.[56]

> They finally got clear of Nish. I think he was fed up with it. He got pensioned off. And, of course, he wasn't there when the mines closed down, because if he had been, they would have got a better deal. I know fellers that worked with them for forty years, and they got pensioned off for seventy dollars. It wasn't a pension, it was nothing. If Nish hadda been around, that would have changed, the men would have got a more equitable pension.

Eric has some well-formed opinions on Unions and what makes a good Union leader. He had mined coal in Nova Scotia in his younger days and had in-laws who were coal miners all their lives. He had returned to Bell Island from Nova Scotia because he had no patience with all the strikes that were constantly interrupting the work there:

> A Union is a good thing. But you must have a good common-sense executive. You've got to have a man who knows where to go and how to stop. Nish Jackman drank more rum than all them Nova Scotian Union leaders put together, but Nish Jackman was a good Union man. And when he went in to look for something, he went in for his men, not himself.

After twenty-two years as Union leader, Jackman left Bell Island on October 3, 1964 to spend his retirement years with his children in Montreal. He died there only three years later in 1967.

THREE

TRAGEDIES IN THE TICKLE

It was like the end of the world.

Ron Pumphrey

DURING WORLD WAR II there were three significant events involving vessels in Conception Bay which profoundly affected the inhabitants of Bell Island. German submarines sank ore boats on two occasions, the first at midday and the second in the early morning. During the second attack, the Island shook when a torpedo hit the pier, shocking most inhabitants out of their sleep. Some people remember only this attack, perhaps because of the jarring effect in the middle of their night's sleep, but in their recollections of the event, have actually blended factors from the two occasions.

Prior to these unusual occurrences, two ferries collided in the Tickle between Portugal Cove and the Island, resulting in the loss of twenty-two people, most of them commuting miners. Most of those questioned remember the collision as having been caused by poor visibility due to a snow squall, and some believe the boats were running without proper lighting because of the blackout imposed by the war. However, as will be seen from the following summary of the official inquiry into the accident, the lighting problems should have been corrected, the snow had stopped when the ferries embarked on their crossings, and the sky remained clear throughout.

The Collision of the *W. Garland* and the *Little Golden Dawn*

On November 10, 1940 at about 5:30 p.m., the *W. Garland*, which was used as a passenger ferry between Portugal Cove and Bell Island, left Portugal Cove with twenty-four passengers plus the captain and engineer on board. As it was a Sunday afternoon, most of the passengers were miners returning after spending the weekend at their homes around Conception Bay. The evening was dark but clear, with occasional snow flurries and a moderate wind from the northeast. The *W. Garland* did not have a passenger-carrying license and was not equipped with life belts. A small life boat that was purchased with the vessel was not carried on it. Only the mast-head light and a search light were working. Bulbs in the port and starboard lights had blown several days earlier. Substitute paraffin lights were available, but the crew did not understand how to install them and their attempts to do so had failed.

At about 5:40 p.m., the *Little Golden Dawn*, another passenger ferry on the same route, left Bell Island with only the captain and engineer on board. This vessel was licensed to carry freight and passengers. There were life belts on board but no life boats. The captain observed the lights of the *W. Garland* approaching from some distance, but neglected to check its compass bearings at regular intervals. Both ferries had each other in clear view, unobstructed by snow flurries. About a quarter of a mile from Bell Island it became obvious that they were going to collide, but the captain of the *Little Golden Dawn* did not blast a warning because his sound signal was not in working order. Instead of pulling to starboard, which is recommended procedure, he pulled to port. At the same time, the captain of the *W. Garland* pulled to starboard and crashed into the starboard side of the *Little Golden Dawn*.

The engineer of the *W. Garland*, who was also the owner, was below in the cabin taking the fares when the collision occurred. While the passengers in the cabin all ran to get out, the owner shouted, "Take your time and see what happens." One passenger responded with, "It is too late to take your time now. The whole head is gone out of her." The stem went into the water quickly, and the passengers rushed for the back of the boat. One man got his pant leg caught in the wheel chain and block during the commotion. He broke the wheelhouse glass with his fist and turned the wheel a half-turn towards him to free himself. He and the owner and two other passengers survived by holding onto debris and were eventually picked up by a rowboat from the Island, which was manned by three men, including Fred Snow, owner of the *Little Golden Dawn*.

It was less than four minutes from the time of the collision until the *W. Garland* sank. The Marine Court Inquiry into the disaster was told that her wood was rotten and she was unseaworthy. Twenty-one passengers and the captain drowned. The *Little Golden Dawn* did not sink right away. Immediately after the collision, the engineer shut off the engine. Then he went back on deck and got hold of the stem of the *W. Garland* in an attempt to hold her in the wound of the *Little Golden Dawn*. When this idea failed, he could not get the engine started again. He and the captain put on life belts and proceeded to pump the water that was entering the boat. About forty-five minutes later, a motor boat towed them to shore, where the ferry quickly sank.[57]

Most of the victims were known and are still remembered by Bell Islanders, as many of them boarded at the homes of residents. One non-resident miner had a shack on the Island that he lived in during the week. Each weekend he went home to be with his family. Every Sunday when he returned, he would go to a neighbour's house for a kettle of water. On the Sunday in question he did not show up. The neighbours became concerned and later learned that he had been among the victims.[58]

Torpedoing of Ore Boats at Bell Island

During the early 1930s, Bell Island miners experienced the effects of the Depression as did other Newfoundlanders. Many men were laid off due to lack of markets for iron ore, and those who were kept on could get only two shifts a week. In the latter part of the 30s, however, things improved greatly as Germany bought more and more iron ore. A week after the last German ore boat left Bell Island, Germany invaded Poland and precipitated World War II. Some products of that iron ore were to return to Wabana a few years later in the form of submarines and torpedoes. Never losing their sense of humour, Bell Islanders joked that "the Nazis were throwing back what they had bought a few years before."[59]

The first attack came about by accident. In August 1942, a German U-boat proceeded to the Strait of Belle Isle.[60] Its mission was to seek out and destroy Allied shipping in the North Atlantic but, after ten days of patrolling the entrance to the Gulf of St. Lawrence to no avail, it moved south. It followed the *Evelyn B.*, a coal boat, into Conception Bay where three loaded ore boats were at anchor between Little Bell Island and Lance Cove, Bell Island, waiting for a convoy to accompany them to their destinations.[61] The submarine waited out the night on the ocean floor. Eric Luffman recalls:

> Jack Harvey had a garden on the back of the Island.
> He was blasting foreman in No. 4. Some nights he

used to go down and stay in his garden all night because there was fellers stealing his cabbage and that. And he was right alongside the edge of the cliff on the back of the Island because there was good soil over there. And this morning was a very foggy morning. And when the fog lifted, this submarine was off the back of the Island. So he immediately went over [to St. John's] and reported it. They kept him there all day. And on the last of it, someone rang up from [Canadian military headquarters in] St. John's and asked Head Constable Russell if there had been any insanity in this feller's family that he knew of. The devil got into Jack. He said, "You go to hell. And if I ever see the whole goddamn German army coming again, they can come in and eat ya." That was the submarine that sunk the first boats a couple of days after, twelve o'clock in the day.

Around noon on September 5, 1942, the Germans discharged a volley of torpedoes at the ore carrier, *S.S. Lord Strathcona*, but the battery switch had not been set to fire, and the torpedoes passed beneath the Customs boat and sank without exploding. The submarine surfaced briefly and was spotted by the gunners of the *Evelyn B.*, who opened fire, hitting the periscope. The submarine disappeared again and fired on the *S.S. Saganaga*, sinking it. The Customs boat went to its aid and picked up five survivors. Small boats from Lance Cove also headed for the scene. The crew of the *Lord Strathcona*, realizing their danger, abandoned their ship and went to help the *Saganaga* survivors. Thirteen men were rescued.

In the confusion, the *Lord Strathcona* swung about, hitting the submarine's conning tower, from which the steering and firing are directed when the submarine is on or close to the surface. The U-boat recovered quickly and sank the *Lord Strathcona*. The

Evelyn B. left the area and headed out the bay, once again unknowingly providing pilotage for the Germans, who had to go back out to sea in order to repair their damage. In the excitement, they did not have time to reload the torpedoes and, therefore, did not attack the *Evelyn B.* She escaped unharmed.

Most of the crew of the *Saganaga* were from the United Kingdom. Twenty-nine died, but only four bodies were recovered. They were laid out at the police station, where residents came to pay their respects, and were buried at the Anglican cemetery.

Sometime later, the Canadian Navy swung into action but, as can be seen from the following remark, some residents were not impressed:

> So now all the corvettes come in, that lollipop navy the Canadians had, and they went back and forth [for a while], and then it died down again.

Late in October, a brand new submarine left Germany with the specific mission of entering Conception Bay, Newfoundland, to destroy ore boats. German intelligence had decoded a message which stated that at least two boats would be at Bell Island the first week of November. Some of the German crew were chosen specifically because they had navigated the waters around Bell Island during peacetime, when they were there loading iron ore. Eric continues:

> So this morning Joe Pynn was going down on the Ledge fishing, and he saw this submarine on the bottom. [His boat] went over them. So he come back in and reported it. And it got that bad that they were going to put him away. And Joe Pynn, he got that mad, he called them down to the dirt. And that night they sunk the boats up there. That was the bunch [Canadian military personnel] over in St. John's over in the

Newfoundland Hotel. They done all their business there, and if you disturbed them at all you were likely to be put in the Lunatic [Asylum].

The attack took place on November 2, 1942 at 3:30 in the morning. A torpedo, aimed at a Greek ship, the *S.S. Anna T.*, which was at anchor off the Scotia pier, missed its target and hit the pier instead. The explosion resounded throughout the Island, jolting the residents from their sleep. Ron Pumphrey was an impressionable eleven-year old:

> I was in bed and there was this great shudder of the house. And I was practically thrown out of bed, it was that kind of shudder. And I know that suddenly I was standing up anyway. It was like the end of the world, you know.

George Picco remembers:

> They meant to blow up the piers, the submarine did. And they fired a torpedo at the piers to try and blow them up, and the torpedo jumped out of the water and went up and hit the cliff. And the place we lived in, at three o'clock in the morning, shook like that [shakes his hand] when the torpedo went up in the cliff and exploded. Shook Bell Island like that.[62]

> Some people even got up and dressed themselves in their best clothes; they were convinced that the Germans were going to take over the Island.[63]

The first ship sunk was the *S.S. Rose Castle*, a DOSCO ore carrier that had been hit by a faulty torpedo only a few weeks earlier while travelling in a Wabana-Sydney convoy.[64] Among the twenty-eight crew members who died was James Fillier of Bell Island, who had joined the ship that very day. Nearby was the Free French ship, *PLM 27*, owned by the British Ministry of Transportation. Its crew were members of the Free French Merchant Navy, most of whom were North Africans. This ship sent up a flare that lit up the area and was probably its undoing, as it was immediately sunk by another torpedo. Twelve of its fifty-member crew died.

Even though the ships were closer to the Island than those of the September incident, rescue work was difficult because of the darkness and the fact that most people had been sleeping. Four men, who were rescued and taken to homes in Lance Cove, died there. Three others had been unconscious when brought ashore, but were revived. In all, fifty-three survivors were given aid on the Island. Twelve bodies were recovered and were laid out at the police station, where the residents, including those as young as Ron was, once again came to pay their respects:

> I remember going down and seeing the bodies in the Court House. Black men who were pale in death and who had cotton wool up their nostrils, and whose faces haunted me for a long time because I'd never seen that kind of thing.

They were buried in the Anglican and Roman Catholic cemeteries. After the war, the bodies of the Free French were taken back to their homeland for reburial. In total, sixty-nine people were killed in the two incidents.

> After that they put a net around the place, you see, and anything that come in it would get caught in the net. But that was too late. They should have put that there after the first [attack], you see, and they would have sove all those lives and those boats.
>
> The Canadian Navy showed up and encircled both

piers with giant steel nets, which served to protect the ore boats while loading and as a haven for smaller craft, mine sweepers and corvettes, when in port. The whole operation was known as the "boom defence," and it was aptly named, since those employed with the Navy enjoyed higher wages than the mines ever paid.[65]

A folk belief, similar to the commonly held belief in ghost ships as ill omens, arose as a result of the ore boat sinkings. After November 2, 1942, some people claimed to have seen one or the other of the ships that had been sunk that night and took it as an omen that they were going to die soon.[66] One woman recalls her own sighting of a "ghost" ship and how she dealt with it:

> The *PLM* went down off Lance Cove at about 3:00 a.m. Not long after, maybe a few days, I came downstairs at about 3:00 a.m. to shake up the fire. And when I looked out the window, I saw the *PLM* all lit up and fully rigged. I never got frightened, but the next day I went to see the priest and told him what I had seen. He asked me if I believed it and I said, "Yes." Then I gave the priest some money to have a mass said for all those on board who had been drowned. I never saw the boat after that.[67]

FOUR

THE MINERS

You've got to make a miner,
and you make him the hard way.

Eric Luffman

ERIC LUFFMAN WAS born on Pilley's Island in Notre Dame Bay, Newfoundland, on May 5, 1905. His father, Stewart Luffman, was a miner there and had also mined in Cobalt, Ontario and shovelled coal in New Aberdeen and Caledonia, both near Glace Bay, Nova Scotia. Like many other Pilley's Island men, Stewart brought his family to Wabana after the iron pyrites mine there closed in March, 1908. He first went to work as a driller for the Dominion Company. In 1912, he became a drill foreman with the Scotia Company, drilling the new submarine slope which was to become No. 3 Mine. Eric's paternal grandfather had also worked on the Island as a boss-carpenter for Dominion. On August 22, 1916, Stewart Luffman was killed by an explosion in the slope. He was 35 years old and the father of six children ranging in age from six months to 13 years. In those days "relief was starvation, so a widow had no chance." Thus, in October 1916, at eleven years of age, Eric went to work to help support his mother and five siblings:

When my father was killed, my mother got two dollars a quarter from the government, eight dollars a year. That was a widow's allowance. She got twenty-five dollars a month from the Company until she got fifteen hundred dollars.

Eric's first job was running messages and keeping time for the surface crew. He did this for two years, making ten cents an hour. He worked ten hours a day, six days a week, from Monday to Saturday. Later he worked at No. 3 Mine, keeping account of the timber going down into the mine. He also measured all the lumber that was used in the buildings that were being constructed: the main hoist, the dry house and the boiler room. Markets were bad in 1923 so the Company laid off all the single men. 18-year old Eric decided to go to Nova Scotia with a fellow who had relatives working there.

Actually there was a history of Conception Bay men going to Nova Scotia to work in the coal mines. It had been reported in 1900 that there was a shortage of workmen on Bell Island because many of them had gone to Sydney to work. The Scotia Company actively recruited men from the area over the years, so it is not surprising that these two young men knew other people who were already working there.[68]

Eric found Sydney to be a "beehive of activity, the hub of eastern Canada." At first he worked in a tar plant in Sydney, tarring logs. Then he got a job in a coal mine in Glace Bay. He might have stayed there, but there were a lot of strikes in the coal mines at that time. In January 1924, less than a year after he arrived there, the men went on strike, so he got work in the lumber woods around Murray Bay until the strike ended. He also went to western Canada that year for the harvest, which was late starting, so he worked with the railway in the meantime, returning to the coal mines after the harvest was over. The coal was low seam, only three and a half feet high, so he was crouched over all day, making it very hard work on the back. Eric laughs when he says, "When I went home the first day, I had to eat my supper under the table." He couldn't straighten up after spending all day bent over in the mines.

He met his wife, Stella, when he boarded at her father's house during his work in the lumber woods. They married just after another big strike started in 1925. He was twenty and she was eighteen. He could not see any sense to all the striking. It seemed to him that the coal miners had nothing else on their minds, so he returned to Bell Island, got a job in the mines and sent for his new bride.

During the Depression, the Wabana miners were only getting two shifts a week. Eric was a driller by this time, making about nine dollars a week. To augment his income, and because there was nothing else to do, he worked for a local farmer when he was not in the mines. For this work he was given a dollar a day plus enough potatoes for the winter, lamb when one was slaughtered, chicken, eggs, milk, and pork when a pig was killed. Some called him a sucker for doing such work, but he was glad to have it. He worked as a driller for fourteen years:

> You would get your work down to perfection so that your work is light, what might be a hard day's work for somebody else, but you know all the tricks of the trade. You make your work light, especially on a drill. You learn every trick and your work is easy. It's when you don't know how to do it that your work is hard.

When Eric started work at age 11, he had little education. After he started working, he took advantage of the Company-operated night school and did very well. By 1939, he had worked his way up to section foreman in No. 3 Mine. This meant he was in charge of one section in one area of the mine. He was made overman of all of one side of the mine in 1940.

Around 1945, he became assistant mine captain and, in 1946, he was made mine captain of No. 3.

In 1965, the year before the mines closed, there was great concern caused by the increase in accidents in the mines. The Union and the Company were in agreement that Eric was the best man to be in charge of safety, to try to cut out the accidents and cut down on the costs:

> I was mine captain for a great many years, a lot of years. I was off sick for a while and, when I came back, Southey said to me, "I got a new job for you." So I wanted to know what was wrong with the job I was doing. He said, "Nothing in the world. I want you to stop the accidents and watch the boys in No. 3 Mine." The last year No. 3 worked, we had three fatal accidents and thirteen more men broke up.

When the shut-down was announced, Eric tore down the two-storey home that he had built and raised his family in on Bell Island and rebuilt it as a bungalow in Portugal Cove, on land where he had formerly had a summer house. His two daughters and their husbands, both of whom had worked at Wabana, built next door. Stella moved to their new home in 1966, but he stayed on the Island for two years after the mines closed, working for the Newfoundland government, selling off mining equipment. He stayed in a shack on the Beach at the front of the Island. He would like to have kept the shack when he was through with his job, to maintain a connection with the place, but he had to sell it:

> Sorriest thing I ever did in my life. But it was no good. I couldn't keep it in repair. It was in bad shape, broke into a couple of times. The neighbour man got afraid somebody would set afire to it alongside his fish place there.

He retired then at the age of 62, after 51 years of service:

> I had to retire. I knew nothing in the world only mining. So it was just as well. I couldn't do anything else.

By age 84, Eric had had plenty of time to ponder his life as a miner. He summed up his working experience very simply:

> Mining is an interesting job, you know. You gotta learn something. First going in the mines, one morning, going back when I was a boy, it struck my mind, good God, am I going to have to come down here every day for the rest of my life? And it got so bad I had a mind to jump off [the man tram] and go home. And if I had, I'd a never gone down there anymore. But then you forget that, and you finally get to a spot when you know this is what's to be. Because we got laid off in 1923, bunch of young men, and I went to a coal mine. I had no job. I got hired on the first thing. But, there's certain things you learn. You must never take a gamble on it. I saw too many accidents of good men. A lot of accidents happened that should never have happened, just because, well, [someone took] a chance. That's one thing you cannot do underground, take a chance.

*　*　*　*　*

George Picco was born January 21, 1911 in Portugal Cove, Conception Bay. For a time his father, Nathan, had commuted to Bell Island to work, but he moved the family there to live when George was a few years old. George was in his early teens, about to take grade six examinations, when he left school to take a job on the picking belt at No. 6 Mine for sixteen cents an hour. He went to work at that time because the family was a large one and needed the extra income. Everyone who could get work took the opportunity. He had an older brother who had started work at age 10. After George had worked at No. 6 for several years, his father got him a job on the No. 3 picking belt.

His next job was on No. 3 marsh on the hind grips, locking the loaded cars to the main cable to take them out to the pier. Steel cable ran right from No. 6 bottom across the Island to the pier. There the cars would be ungripped from the main rope to go into the tipple, which tipped the cars over so that all the ore would go down in the pockets. He worked on the Scotia line for a few years, but each winter the line would close down, and the ore was stock-piled at the mine surface until spring. Because he did not like being laid off each fall, he got a job in No. 2 Mine shovelling iron ore, which he describes as being hard work:

> I stood it out for six or eight months. I'd have two or three [new] buddies every week, strange buddies, and I was nearly broke up. The last thing, I gave it up. Got a job on the surface, on No. 2 deckhead.

George continued to work at No. 2 deckhead for a while. Then he heard that men were needed for No. 4 Mine to keep the small cars in repair. These cars ran in twelve-car trips up and down No. 2 and No. 4 Mines. He got a job in the No. 4 car shop and worked there for some years. Next he went to work in No. 3 car shop working on the twenty-ton cars which brought the ore out of No. 3 Mine. He worked there for years before moving on to the machine shop. At first his work involved helping different men and cleaning up. Then he worked at sawing off long pieces of iron. He worked as a drill press operator for a long time before going on to the threading machine, threading pipes of various diameters. He was 55 years old and still working at the machine shop when news came of the closure of the operations.

He had only left Bell Island once to look for work elsewhere, and that was one time when the mines closed for three or four months. Like many other men from all over Newfoundland, he and a friend went to seek work at the United States naval base which was under construction in Argentia. There they did "pick and shovel work" until the mines opened up again.

When he learned, in April 1966, that the mines were to close down for good in June, he decided not to wait until the end to look for a job. He thought he might have trouble getting one then with so many other people also looking, so he took a few days off work and went to St. John's, where his eldest daughter was living. He went to see the superintendent at McNamara Industries on Topsail Road and asked him for a job. George had never had any formal training and had no diplomas, so he had never thought of himself as having a trade as such. Thus, when he described the work he had been doing in the machine shop on Bell Island, he felt quite proud when the superintendent at McNamara's told him that he had a good trade. "You can call it that if you like," was George's reply. As it happened, they needed a man to work on their big electric drill, so he started work there the very next day. His wife, Sarah, and their youngest daughter stayed on the Island until the end of October. Then they rented out their home there and moved to St. John's. They received the standard $1,500 resettlement grant from the provincial government, which had been offering the same amount to anyone in Newfoundland who would be willing to leave small, economically depressed areas to live in larger centres. Several different families rented the Picco's house before George got tired of making repairs and gave up his dream of one day retiring to it. Finally, he sold the house for $6,000.

* * * * *

Harold Kitchen was born in Harbour Grace, Conception Bay, on October 24, 1914. His father, Harvey, worked on Bell Island in the Scotia barn, looking after the horses that were used in the mines. He moved his family to Bell Island from Harbour Grace in 1922 when Harold was seven years old.

Harold remembers well the trip to the Island and his first impressions of it. They travelled in a motor boat and, after landing at the Beach on the east side of the Island, were taken up the steep hill in the passenger tram car that was pulled by an engine-driven cable. Harold's father made a phone call from the tramway station for transportation. They were then picked up by a horse-drawn, covered wagon. The driver sat out front on a very high seat and held a long whip in his hand. The cost of the ride to their new home on the Scotia Ridge was fifty cents each for the two adults, while the four children rode free.

On October 8, 1928, sixteen days before his fourteenth birthday, Harold went to work with the Company. He had attended school until then and had attained grade six. His first job was on the picking belt of No. 2 Mine, picking rock out of the iron ore as it came out of the mine. There was a house over the picking belt, but the bottom was all open. It was fifty feet or more up in the air, with chutes that the boys threw the rocks down into. The wind blew up through these chutes, making it very cold working there. He "suffered it out" for over a year just to have a job, for which he was paid nineteen cents an hour.

The Depression caused a temporary closing of No. 2 Mine in 1930, so Harold went to No. 3, boiling kettles in which the men warmed their bottles of tea. His next job was in the office of No. 6 Mine, sending supplies into the mines, answering the telephone and running messages. Around 1936, he went into No. 6 Mine, driving hoists and running trips. He worked there until 1943. That year the mines were closed all winter, so he went to St. Lawrence and worked in the fluorspar mines, going back to Bell Island again when the mines there reopened. On two other occasions he went to work at the naval base in

Surface mining c. 1895 when the operation was exclusively above ground.

In February 1920, miners at 900' west level, No. 6 Mine, pose with a Myers Whaley shovel. This shovel was used on a trial basis for a short time but was found to break down too often. Note the hand shovels hung along the wall. The men are wearing carbide lamps on their caps, while the man on the right holds a glenny lamp, used for testing for methane gas.

With No. 3 deckhead in the background, miners wait for the man rake to take them underground. Starting on the left and moving right, some of the men in this photograph are: Dennis Murphy, Dick Sutton, Tom Brazil, Chris Parsley, Norm Reynolds, John Parsons(?), Bill Ford, George Kearley(?), George Churchill(?), Bill Bursey, Frank Fitzgerald, Solomon Rees. The rectangular device the man on the left front is holding is the battery pack for his electric lamp, which is lying on the ground in front of him.

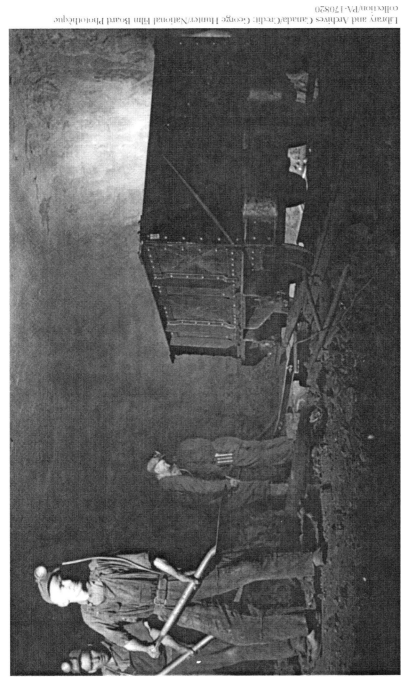

Jim Slade (?) and Edgar Parsons hand load iron ore into an ore car at 900' west level, No. 3 Mine, while two trackmen in the background lay track to bring the car in closer to the muck, August 1949.

An 1800-pound mine horse hauls an empty four-ton ore car to the face for loading at the 900' west level, No. 3 Mine, August 1949, with teamster Bill Pynn at the reins. The two loaders behind him are Edgar Parsons and Jim Slade(?). While the men were loading the car, a sprag placed in the wheel kept the car from rolling away. When loading was finished, the sprag was removed and the car would run down the two-percent grade on its own. The horse would then haul in another car to be loaded.

Lunch time underground in a dry house in No. 3 Mine, August 1949. The three men facing are Tommy Reynolds (pouring water), Rube Rowe and Jack Pendergast. Note the lunches hung on the wall out of the reach of the rats and the large bottle of tea warming on the stove. An important function of the oil burner was to keep water warm in case it was needed in the event of an accident.

67

Bill Jardine, who was overman of the west side of No. 3 Mine, has his midmorning "mug up" in the foreman's shack, August 1949. The bottle contains tea sweetened at home with milk and sugar. The brown paper that holds his lunch is on the bench next to him.

Miners coming off shift wait for the tram to take them to the surface, August 1949. Left to right: Tom Murphy, Jimmy Kavanagh, Fred Ezekiel, Austin Clark, Lewellyn Hutchings, Tommy Reynolds, Richard Swain, Bill Ryan(?), Mose Penny, --- Smith, unidentified.

69

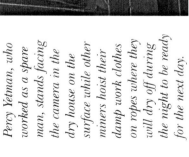

Percy Yetman, who worked as a spare man, stands facing the camera in the dry house on the surface while other miners hoist their damp work clothes on ropes where they will dry off during the night to be ready for the next day.

Lunch time, September 1948. Since they are not wearing lamps or mine caps, these young men are probably working on the surface, perhaps at the pier. Note the water bucket with its cover to keep the dust out, the lunch papers and the long-necked drink bottles.

Argentia for short periods. He had no trouble getting hired back on in the mines after each of these breaks. Another year, when the mines were working only two shifts a week, he went to St. John's and worked in a shoe factory on Job Street for the winter. When he returned to Bell Island this time, however, his former job was gone, so he worked at digging out the basement for the Salvation Army school.

After that he got a job shovelling iron ore. He spent eleven months at this and also "worked at just about every job there was in No. 3 Mine." After working all day in the mines, he would spend his evenings vegetable gardening. In the late 1940s, he took on additional work on a part-time basis as an undertaker's helper, laying out corpses and assisting with accidents in the mines. He continued this part-time work until 1965.

Joy Loaders, machines which loaded ore and, thus, replaced some of the hand-shovellers, were introduced in 1949. Harold was one of the men picked to "come on the surface" to learn how to drive the machines. Then he went back into the mines to teach others how to drive them. A short while after that he was promoted to foreman, a position he held until the mines closed. He worked until the last day of the mining operation in June 1966.

The year before mining ceased, he attended evening classes at the Trades School and earned a grade eleven diploma. After the closure, he returned to the school and learned how to operate diesel equipment. He had been driving electrical equipment in the mines. He then got a job in Dunville, Placentia Bay, for a short period. Following this, he worked at a series of custodial jobs at Memorial University, the St. John's airport and the various hospitals in St. John's.

When they left Bell Island, Harold and his wife, Una, took advantage of a joint federal-provincial scheme whereby they gave up their twenty-nine-year-old home to the provincial government for $1,500. This was the same amount everyone else received who took advantage of this plan, whatever the age or condition of the house. The owner could buy back his home for one dollar with the provision that he tear it down. He could then rebuild it off the Island, and a number of people did this. Some homes that were in poor condition were resold for a dollar each to people who were willing to tear the house down and use the lumber as firewood. The Department of Welfare retained other homes and moved families on social assistance into them. This is what happened to Harold's home.

He could have gotten a pension at the time of the mine closing even though he was only 51years old. It would have been for a very small amount, however, so he drew out the money he had paid into the pension plan and "I finished with Bell Isle."

*   *   *   *   *

Len Gosse was born January 8, 1916 on Bell Island. His father, Bartholomew, who was born in Spaniard's Bay, Conception Bay, had worked in the Tilt Cove copper mines before going to Bell Island in 1910. At Wabana, he was a driller for fifty years and continued working until he was seventy-one. His later years were spent on the surface, "on the deck, firing the big boiler, keeping the steam up."

Len got his very first job at the Dominion Pier when he was in grade five. His father had a small boat tied up at the pier, and Len and a buddy of his would sneak down the back way over the cliff to the boat. The man who was superintendent of both piers, Dominion and Scotia, called to them one day and asked if they wanted a job. He sent them to the office to get a number and then put them to work slacking a rope back and forth on an ore boat that was being loaded.

Len started working in earnest with the Company in September 1928 at age 12. Times were bad as the start of the Depression began to show its effects on the mining operation and, with eleven in his family, the extra income was badly needed. His father was earning $2.20 a day, two days a week. Len and his buddy went to the superintendent of the pier and, perhaps because his buddy's older brother was courting the superintendent's daughter, they were hired on as shovellers. They would work at the pier two days and then spend another two days working on the construction of the United Church parsonage. The superintendent of the pier was working as a carpenter there and the boys worked as his helpers. Between the two jobs, Len was earning $9.60 a week, more than twice what his father was making.

Following this, in 1934, he worked at the last of the surface mines, No. 35, loading iron ore. From 1936 to 1938, he loaded iron ore in No. 2 Mine. He then went back to working on the pier and, in 1939, got married. The pay was not so good at the pier, so he went back working underground. He spent three years pipe-fitting and then worked as a "chucker." A chucker was a man who worked along with a driller, changing the steel in the holes and fetching. As Len put it: "The driller just drilled, but the chucker had to do all the work." He also worked as a "road maker," laying down tracks with sixty-pound railing for the four-ton cars to run on.

The only time he ever considered working off the Island was in 1942, when there was a ten-week lay-off due to slow markets during World War II. After failing to obtain work at Argentia, he returned to Bell Island and was hired as a sales clerk and delivery man in a grocery store.

When the Joy Loaders were introduced in 1949, many men feared for their jobs because these loaders would do the jobs normally done by men. One day the walking boss asked Len if he wanted to go to work on a loader because one of the operators had gotten hurt. He agreed to do it, but was warned that the other men might despise him for taking such a job. Some had refused to work on the loaders because they did not want them in the mines. The next morning, when he got in one of the twelve cars for the trip underground, the men in his car left and sat in other cars to show their displeasure:

> No one would sit in the car with me. That's the way they felt, but it didn't fizz on me.

Len was a "spare foreman" for fourteen years. When the section foreman went on holidays, Len would take his place. When the walking boss took his holidays, the section foreman replaced him and, again, Len would replace the section foreman. Then when the assistant mine captain took his holidays, he was replaced by the walking boss, who was replaced by the section foreman, who, once again, would be replaced by Len.

He also worked at "carrying steel," bringing in various lengths of steel for the drillers to use. It was when he was doing this work that he was given a chance to try his hand at drilling. He continued as a driller until 1958, when he had an accident which left him unable to work for long periods: one day as the shuttle car passed by, going around a turn, it struck a lump of ore which hit Len on his right leg and foot, badly injuring his shin. He spent the next eight years undergoing operations to correct the damage.

When the mines closed down in June 1966, he was 50 years old and off work due to his injury, receiving workmen's compensation of $176 a month. He was attending a meeting, at which badges for twenty-five years service were being presented, when the announcement was made that, "this will be the last badges for twenty-five years service; the mines are closing down next week." The mines actually operated for another two months, but some of the men that Len knew did not bother to go to work the next day. They simply packed their belongings and left for Galt, Ontario, where there was the promise of factory jobs. Hundreds of former Bell Island miners had already made their homes there. Even though his brother had found work in Galt, Len decided to stay on Bell Island, perhaps because of his injury.

Two years later, in June 1968, he decided to try and get a job in St. John's. His daughter knew some people at the Confederation Building who she thought might be able to help, so she went with him and introduced him to them. After some shuffling from one office to another, he went home to Bell Island to await a phone call. At the end of the week, the call came saying that he had a job with security at the Confederation Building.

He had a house on Bell Island which he boarded up. With so many people leaving the Island at that time to find work elsewhere, it was impossible to sell a house for a reasonable price. Also, like many people, he did not want to sell his home because he had hopes of returning to the Island, either when the mines were reactivated or when he retired. Len bought a house on Portugal Cove Road. One day the RCMP came to his door and notified him that his house on Bell Island had been broken into. After going there to survey the damage, he decided it would be best to give up the house. He felt it should have been worth about $10,000, but he sold it to the provincial government for its fixed price of $1,500. Again he went to the Confederation Building, this time to see the man who was in charge of buying homes on Bell Island:

> He said, "You're selling your home?" I said, "Yes."
> "Okay," he told me, and he just wrote out the cheque for $1,500. No more to it than that. And I passed him over the deed.

*   *   *   *   *

Albert Higgins was born on Bell Island on January 2, 1920. His father, Ernest, was a miner who originally came to the Island each Monday to work and returned home each Saturday to Goddenville, near Spaniard's Bay. He moved to the Island permanently when he married. In Goddenville, he had kept cattle for meat. He had also fished on the Labrador. On Bell Island, Ernest Higgins was a driller and, in later years, a blaster.

Albert left school at 13 to work at unloading the coal and freight boats at the pier. In 1936, at 16, he was hired by the Company to work on the picking belt, also called the rubber belt. He put in a ten-hour day, six days a week. He worked on the rubber belt for a year before going on the steel belt. Working on the steel belt was considered a man's job. It involved picking larger rocks from the ore when it first came from the mine. Once the large rocks had been picked out, the ore went through a crusher. It then went on the rubber belt where the younger boys picked the now smaller rocks from it. He later worked on the rock car which hauled away the waste from the iron ore.

He went down in No. 3 Mine as a "spare man" in 1942. This job involved filling in wherever the boss directed. If there was a man off work, the spare man took his place that day. This was full-time work because there was always something to do. One of the jobs he did was "flogging" or "tramming," disconnecting the cables from the empty cars and attaching them to the full ones. From there, the cars were sent back to the headways, or to the lower levels to go out to the "pocket," where the ore was dumped before being taken up out of the mine. After some time at that, he worked at pipe-fitting. He also drove the electric hoist which lowered ore down over the headways to the pocket. He later went to work in the pockets and became foreman there.

Albert left Bell Island only once to look for work elsewhere. In 1943, when the mines closed down for two months in the winter, he got a job doing construction work on the Southside in St. John's. He stayed there for two weeks, but did not like it so he went back to the Island again.

Even when the announcement was made that the mines were closing down, he stayed on and worked to the end. Leading up to the September 1966 provincial election, Premier Smallwood gave assurances that a German company was going to take over the operation, so he stayed on the Island for a few months after the closure. He finally left Bell Island for good in October 1966, when it was announced that the German deal had fallen through. He was 46 years old.

He and his wife, Annie, owned their home on Bell Island and "gave it away" for seven hundred dollars, which was less than the cost of the new bathroom he had recently installed. The Government scheme for buying homes had not yet come into effect. He obtained work in St. John's as a security officer at Memorial University.

*　*　*　*　*

Ron Pumphrey was born February 6, 1931 in Harbour Grace, Conception Bay. His father, Isaac, who was also born in Harbour Grace, went to work on Bell Island as a cook in a mess shack. Ron went there with him at an early age and slept in the kitchen on a bunk that his father made for him of tongue-and-groove board. He recalls one occasion when two men got into a scuffle, and one of them threw a bowl of soup in the other's face:

My father went down the aisle of long tables and, resting one hand on one of the tables, leapt over the table, struck this fellow square in the chest and face with his boots and knocked him out.

He remembers going to Bell Island on the ferry with his father and the other North Shore men after spending the weekend at home. Although his father did not approve, the men would make a game of hiding the child behind them on the bench while the ticket taker went through.

His father later became a Company policeman. He wore a black uniform with brass buttons and a badge that had "Company Police" encircled by a wreath emblazoned on it. The remainder of the family was still living in Harbour Grace while Ron and his father lived in a watchman's shack at No. 6.

At about age 12, Ron worked summertime liming the fences of Company-owned houses. An inspector would be sent around to make sure the boys were doing a good job. The pay rate was a quarter of a cent per paling, which worked out to about ten dollars a week. He also worked on the coal boats that came into the pier, before getting a job liming the west bottom. This was where the loaded iron ore cars would come and be gripped onto cables for dumping. These were all short-term jobs so, at 15, he asked the foreman, John Charles Vokey, for full-time work. Mr. Vokey gave him a job gripping, along with a lecture about how he should be in school getting his diploma. Ron was attending night school, however, and passed with honours when he was 16. He tells what it was like to be 15 years old gripping ore cars:

> You had this three-feet long, steel, wrench-like object that you put on the front of an iron ore car. You lifted on this large nut on the upper front of the ore car, which brought two iron jaws together underneath the

car to grip a running cable. And you forced up on that until it snapped and then, as the car went ahead, you jumped on the cable at the back of the car while holding on to the car, and with one foot you shoved the cable under the jaws behind the car. And then you placed the wrench-like bar atop the nut in the upper part of the back of the car, and you pushed down on it now to bring the jaws in to grip the running cable. I was pushing up one time on the fore nut, and my scapula caved in on my lung. And I fell forward in a paralytic stupor, and I could hear the nut click loose as the car went ahead on a rise. And I knew the car was coming back, and I tried to move away. And, as I moved away, the car took the sleeve out of my coat. And I couldn't move. The men rushed out and grabbed me and pulled me aside. And I was just there like this [paralysed], and they took me to the clinic. But I was all right the next day.

His next job was "spragging." Spragging was the term given to slowing down the empty ore cars that were released from the cable by the gripper after they had been unloaded at the pier. The empties would come down to be refilled at the stockpile. The spragger would kneel beside a long log on which there were three-foot steel bars, pointed at one end, which were called sprags. Starting at the far left of the log, the spragger, kneeling in a squat position, took two sprags and, as the first car came, threw them with great force at the wheels. The wheels had curved supports for the purpose of accepting the sprags. The car would stagger ahead, and the spragger would continue to sprag the cars coming behind it, the idea being to stop the cars from banging into one other and going off the track.

Ron's career with the Company ended when he was 16. He left Bell Island and took a position with *The Western Star* newspaper in Corner Brook. Some years later, he returned to edit and publish a local weekly newspaper, *The Bell Island Reporter*. In the fall of 1966, after the mines had closed, he was unanimously elected chairman of the Bell Island Economic Improvement Council. This was a group of concerned businessmen who banded together in an effort to attract mining interests to the Island and generally seek ways and means to lessen the detrimental impact that the cessation of mining had on the whole community. He resigned the following summer when it was found that the Newfoundland government would not recognize the Council or co-operate with it. The Council's correspondence with a German firm was then passed over to the Government, but nothing concrete ever came of its efforts to reopen the mines.

After leaving Bell Island, Ron worked in public relations in St. John's. He also spent time as a writer and publisher of a series of Newfoundland who's-who books, a radio talk-show host, a St. John's city councillor, a captain with the Salvation Army, and a business columnist for *The Evening Telegram*.

*   *   *   *   *

Clayton Basha was born March 1, 1937 on Bell Island. His father, George, was a businessman who sold groceries, managed a pinball-machine and pool-table business and did some contract work for DOSCO, such as transporting dynamite. George was born in Grand Falls to Syrian immigrants Ameen and Maria Basha.

When he was growing up, Clayton never imagined himself working in the mines. It was the farthest thing from his mind. He had thought he would like to be an RCMP officer, but he did not do well in school and stopped at grade eight. He worked with his father one summer driving a truck, delivering dynamite for DOSCO. After that summer, he decided he wanted to go to the Trades School in St. John's. His first choice was a mechanical trade, but the course was full so he took welding instead.

When he finished his course, he went to see Jim Archibald, who was superintendent of maintenance. His name was put on file and, after a month or so, he received a call saying there was a vacancy. He was 18 years old when he started in the machine shop on the surface. He worked there for three months to get some experience and to see how things were done. After that, he was sent underground in No. 3 Mine, where he worked for three or four years with the maintenance department. Because he had always enjoyed mechanical work, he took a home study course in his spare time and, upon completing it, was transferred to the mechanical department. He was still involved in much the same work. When he had been welding, if there was no welding to do, he would do mechanical work anyway. His work involved repairing mine equipment such as the Joy Loaders.

He did shift work the same as the regular miners until his department went on "continuous operations." With this system, he might work through a weekend and then be off in the middle of the week for three days. After a while, he would get a long four-day weekend, but then would have to work seven days straight. There was a lot of overtime work. He would spend as much as thirty-six hours at a stretch underground.

He got married when he was twenty-two. The first house that he and his wife, Lillian, bought had been built out of dynamite boxes. For a while, they rented a store on the Green and tried their hand at selling, but that did not work out.

When Clayton started working in 1956, Wabana was at its

peak. It was not long before things started to look bad:

> I really thought, due to the fact that we didn't leave
> the Island that much, that once there was a slow down,
> in regards to losing your job, that there was no other
> job in existence. That's the truth. This was it. This was
> the end.

Even though he saw quite a lot of lay-offs in his 10 years with
the Company, he was never laid off himself. This may have
been due to the trade he had. It was almost right to the end
before he realized that the close-down was coming:

> I couldn't see it coming. I never looked down the
> road. It seems to me that when Lab City and Wabush
> started up, that was the starting of it then. But to
> be honest with you, I could always see light, you
> know, right up until the end. I thought it was going
> to keep going. There would be something start up.
> They were going to put another plant over there and
> make briquettes, to make the ore more valuable, put
> ingredients with it. But that never, ever came true.
> That was only an election dodge, I believe.

He worked off the Island once, and he was still with the
Company even then. About two months before the shut-down,
he was sent to Whalesback copper mine near Springdale. They
used the same equipment as was used at Wabana, and the
Company was hoping to sell some of its equipment to them.
Clayton spent about two weeks there and was offered a job, but
would not take it: "I was scared." (Five years later that mine also
folded.) He stayed working right to the end, June 30, 1966. He
was 29 years old:

> We felt sad. Like I said, you were wondering, what
> else is there? And the funny part about all that, like,

we were bringing home seventy-five dollars a week, and that was a good wage then. And I can remember distinctly the unemployment was thirty-five dollars a week. But still in all, after a week or two, or a month, you got along with that thirty-five dollars just the same as on the seventy-five.

In 1967, he went to Wabush to work for a few months during the winter. "All the while I was in Wabush, it was in the back of my mind that they might close down like Bell Island did." His family stayed on the Island during this time. Then he came back and got a job in St. John's and commuted for about six months. He found this very tiring: "On the go fourteen to sixteen hours a day to get eight hours work." Having to take the ferry twice a day was the biggest problem. He started looking for a place to rent in St. John's, but everything was too expensive. He finally found a place in Torbay for eighty dollars a month. "I just about went crazy then, paying out rent, not used to that, see." Lillian adds, "We wanted to be near a school, not used to the children going on buses." That was 1968. They were renting for exactly two years before they bought their present home.

When they left Bell Island, they rented their home out, but were getting reports of break-ins and other problems, so they eventually sold it and received the government's $1,500 grant:

> When I came over here and I realized, I just about went out of my mind to think that I didn't know no better than to go down in the bowels of the earth to try to make a living. I must have been crazy. See, your life wasn't worth a nickel when you stop to think about it.

FIVE

The Working Life

*I didn't know no better than to go down in the
bowels of the earth to try to make a living.*

Clayton Basha

THE MAJORITY OF the men who went underground at Wabana, whether a shoveller, a driller, or a mine captain, had many experiences in common. Most of them shared the same taste in food, wore the same kind of clothing and started out in the industry under similar circumstances. As the main reason to begin working in the first instance was to obtain money with which to support themselves and their families, it seems fitting to begin this chapter with a look at wages over the years.

Wages
I am killing myself for 10 c./H.

Miners were making ten cents an hour in 1896. The strike of 1900 resulted in a raise to eleven cents for ordinary labourers and twelve and a half cents for skilled miners. A boy's pay was ten cents an hour when Eric Luffman started working for the mining operation in 1916, while men shovelling iron ore were receiving thirteen cents an hour. By the time Harold Kitchen started working twelve years later, in 1928, boys were earning nineteen cents an hour. Len Gosse recalled that his father, who was a driller, was earning twenty-two cents an hour that year. However, the Depression brought poor markets, so the men worked only two days a week and his father's week's pay was a mere $4.40. A man's pay had risen to thirty-two cents an hour by 1936.

Miners were paid a "war bonus" during World War II. The amount depended on what each man was earning. "Road makers," who laid down track for the ore cars to run on, and "teamsters," who handled the horses, got thirty dollars, paid over a year. Drillers, who earned more, received forty dollars, and foremen received more still.

During the 1950s, regular miners brought home thirty dollars a week. Harold was a foreman and was making $480 a month when the mines closed in 1966. This was considered good pay at that time. By comparison, when he got a job doing security work at the General Hospital in St. John's a few years later, he was paid only $200 a month.

At one time, the men were paid every fortnight. They were paid by cheque, but they had a basic distrust of this method of payment and, in 1925, asked to be paid in cash. From then on, they each received a small, brown envelope with their weekly pay in cash inside. Any deductions were written on the back of the envelope. People who lived in Company-owned houses had deductions made for rent, electricity and coal. Other deductions taken out of everyone's envelope were taxes, thirty cents a month for the doctor, two percent for support of churches and, in later years, unemployment insurance.

Monday was payday in the 1930s and 40s. However, the Company changed that to Tuesday when it was found that some men came to work on Monday just to get paid and then took the rest of the day off for an extended weekend. Friday was payday in the later years. The shops remained open during the evening on that day and, after supper, the grocery and other shopping was done.

Working Hours

If she was working six days a week,
we wouldn't see daylight until Sunday.

When Eric's father started working at Wabana in 1910, there were two shifts a day, six days a week. The men worked a ten-hour day, which actually involved eleven hours because the dinner hour was on the workers' own time. The ten-hour day was changed later to include the dinner hour. The drillers would go down on the day shift to drill, and the blasters would go down for the night shift to do the blasting.

For the ten-hour shift, the work itself began at seven o'clock, but the men had to be ready to board the man trams to go into the mines when the Company whistle blew at six forty-five.[69] In the fall, it would be dark when the men went down in the morning and dark again when they came back up at the end of the shift. When the mine worked the full six days a week, the day shift workers would not see daylight until Sunday, their day off. Once a month, the men also had Saturday off. They would work six days for three weeks, and then the next week was a five-day week. The idea was to give the men who resided on the mainland a long weekend home with their families.

The shift ended for the men shovelling iron ore when they had their twenty "boxes," or ore cars, loaded. Two men loaded twenty boxes a day between them. They could load more and get overtime pay but, as a rule, the men who resided on Bell Island would call it a day when they had their complement.

However, a lot of miners were not residents. Some boarded with residents, others had small shacks, while many lived in Company-owned "mess shacks" during the week. They all went home to their families around Conception Bay on weekends. The mess shacks held thirty men each, and each bunk had a mattress stuffed with hay:

> The bed fleas could almost carry you away. You would be awake almost all night killing bedbugs and, oh, what a smell when you killed them.

These men were known by several names: "baymen," "main-landsmen," "mainland fellers," and "mainlanders" or, as a lot of them came from the north shore of Conception Bay, "North Shore men." Ironically, when their buses pulled into their home communities on the weekends, people there would say, "here come the Bell Isle men."[70]

When the mines worked six days a week, Friday for these men was "preparation day," and Saturday was "rush day," or "scravel day." On a normal day, each pair of men hand-loaded twenty boxes of ore, and perhaps a few extra to go towards Saturday's complement of twenty boxes. On Fridays, a special effort was made to load as many extra cars as possible in "preparation" for the next day. Then, on Saturday mornings, they often would go down into the mines earlier than usual and "rush" to finish loading enough to make up their twenty boxes for that day. As soon as that was accomplished, they could leave for home. Harold recalls a popular Bell Island story that was associated with scravel day:

> An Island Cove man named Jim Adams was coming up early from the mine when he met Tommy Gray, the supervisor, who said to him, "You're up early today." "Yes, Old Man," Adams answered, "I was sot (ie. planted) early." "What happened to your buddy?

Wasn't he sot early too?" asked Mr. Gray. "Oh yes, sir," said Adams, "but the grubs cut he off."

The mainlanders would also load extra cars for extra pay. The men would leave the deck to enter the mines at six forty-five a.m., get off the trams at seven and arrive at the working face, ready to start loading, at seven fifteen. In the room where they were working, there would probably be six empty cars on the siding. Each car could hold a ton and a quarter. Once those six cars were loaded, they would be pushed out and another six would be drawn in. There would be three six-car trips to be loaded, plus two cars from the next six-car trip. Then there would be four cars left over. Since the mainland men had nothing to look forward to when they finished work for the day, except killing time in the mess shack, they would often stay underground and load the extra four cars, getting twenty cents extra pay for each car.

Changes in the work day came about with the advent of the Union in the 1940s. When the eight-hour day was achieved in 1943, shifts ran from eight a.m. to four p.m., known as the "day shift," four p.m. to midnight, known as the "four o'clock shift," and midnight to eight a.m., known as the "back shift" or the "graveyard shift." The drillers' routine then became one in which they spent the first part of the shift drilling and the second part blasting. They spent five days on day shift, five on the four o'clock shift and five nights on the back shift.

Retiring and Pensions

I know a man, when he started retirement, he was over eighty.

Men did not retire from the mining operation until the late years when, sometime in the 1950s, one of the managers "started retiring people." Before that, men simply kept working until old age or failing health prevented them from doing so any longer. One man was working on the picking belt when he was over eighty years old. When he had become less fit to work in the mines, he had been put back to the lighter job that he had done as a boy. When he could no longer do that work, he was pensioned at twenty dollars a month. Another man, who had been working in the mines for forty years when the mines closed down, received a pension of forty-seven dollars a month.

Paid vacations were not a part of the miner's life until the Union won that benefit in the 1950s. Most men only got two weeks off, and the whole operation would shut down for that period. Everybody would be off except for the men working on the pumps. The water would have to be kept pumped out so that the mines would not flood.

Foodways

We used to have a frying pan and fry up onions in the night.

In earlier years, the men ate lunch wherever they could find a dry place to sit down. In later years, they made up lunch rooms, which were actually not much more than a "hole in the rock." The lunch rooms were called "dry houses," a name also used for the change houses on the surface. Since the bottom in the mines ran at an angle all the way down, sticks were put across and planks laid on top of them to make a level room. There were benches all around the room for the men to sit on to eat their lunches. There was usually an old oil stove and a large boiler to warm water in. For many years, men were employed to keep the water boiling. These were often older or injured men who could no longer do hard labour. The miners would put their bottles of tea in the boilers to keep them hot. Anyone who had a can of soup or such could also heat it up in the boiler. For the men who worked on the surface, boys were employed to boil kettles and fetch water. These boys were called "nippers."

There were no breaks for the men underground until they stopped to eat their lunch. Up until the eight-hour shift was introduced in 1943, for the day shift the men went down at seven a.m. and worked until eleven or twelve o'clock before breaking to eat what they referred to as "dinner," the same as the midday meal at home was called. The men working the four o'clock shift and the graveyard shift called their lunch break "supper," the same as the evening meal at home was called. For the men drilling on the back shift, there was a certain amount of drilling that would have to be done. Then all the men would go into the dry house for their supper. "Probably that would be four o'clock in the morning but we called it supper anyway."

In the 1930s, at nine a.m., after having been at work for two hours, the boys on the picking belt would take turns having their break. They called it a "mug-up." At noon they had dinner. There was another mug-up at three o'clock. There was a set amount of time that each person had for dinner, but for the mug-ups "you had to scravel and get right back to work."

It was usually the miner's wife who "rigged," or prepared, his lunch, either in the morning before he left for work or the previous night. Common lunch items were sandwiches, which were often made of baloney, since it was the cheapest meat or, instead of sandwiches, buttered bread accompanied by such items of food as small tins of beans or sardines, fried sausages, "black" or "blood" puddings, ham, meat, fish cakes or meat cakes. To top off the meal, there would be a small can of fruit or juice. Flat tins of pineapple chunks were popular with the young fellows. Clayton Basha recounts the method miners used for holding a slice of bread in their ore-covered hands:

> When you were eating a slice of bread, you'd take it by a corner. You had no way of washing up. You couldn't wash up for lunch. There was no sinks. There was no

nothing. So you'd have the piece of bread, I think I even used to do it at home out of fashion, you'd grab hold of one corner of the bread, and that's the way you'd eat it. Then you'd heave the corner away.

Besides the officially sanctioned breaks and the normal food items, there were other times, usually during the night shifts, when the men would have special things to eat. For example, when Harold was a young man, if he was working the back shift and his parents happened to be out somewhere for the evening, when they were going home they would stop by with some chocolate bars as a treat for him. Some men would have a frying pan in their dry house and, occasionally, they would fry onions for a snack. There were a couple of maintenance men, a mechanic and electricians, who had a shack of their own. It was said of them that they used to cook "feeds" on Company time.

The men used various containers for carrying their lunch to work. In the early years of mining, the men used a gallon lunch can which was round like a paint can with a wire handle. The handle could be pulled up over the arm for easy carrying, much like a lady's handbag. There were nails in the dry house to hang the lunch cans on to keep them out of the reach of rats. These cans were specially made up in the tinsmith shop. At lunch time, the can could be filled with boiling water and loose tea steeped in it. Some men carried their lunch in paper bags. The men from Freshwater, a community at the south-western end of the Island, were noted for their custom of having their lunches wrapped in brown paper which they then put into big red and blue pocket handkerchiefs. When they went into the mines, they would hook these handkerchiefs on nails in a post along the rib, again, to keep them out of reach of the rats.

There was always fresh water available to the men while they worked. This was brought down in large cans. Most men took a bottle of tea down to drink with lunch. As already mentioned, the tea bottle was heated in a boiler in the dry house. Some men would rest the tea bottle against the rib while they shovelled, preferring the cold tea as a thirst quencher when they became overheated with the strenuous work. The most popular "tea bottle" was an empty rum flask. The flask was filled with tea, which was often sweetened with sugar and canned milk at home, and then corked. The cork was attached to the bottle neck by a string. In the following humorous story, which circulated on the Island for a while, it seems that the miner involved must have been in the habit of leaving the cork out of his empty flask. It is reported that it was always told as a true experience and, in many instances, the man was named:

A certain miner had recently started working on the four o'clock shift. He had some cows which he had put to pasture in Kavanagh's Meadow, a lonely, level stretch of land at the east end of the Island and, since starting this new shift, was forced to go round them up when he got off work at midnight. Though the landscape was foreboding enough, the man was especially frightened by strange sounds which he had been hearing ever since he started doing this late night roundup. He was so anxious to get the job over with as quickly as possible that he would start to run as soon as he reached the meadow. On this night, he reached the pasture and had no sooner started running than the eerie whistling began once again. The faster he ran, the louder the noise became, and he was convinced that it was the horrible moan of a restless spirit that was chasing him. He was just coming within sight of his cows when the man tripped. As he lay motionless on the ground, he noticed the sounds had ceased. At the same time, he felt an uncomfortable bulge in his back pocket and pulled out his tea flask. Only then did he realize that the wind blowing over the mouth of the flask was the cause of those unearthly sounds.[71]

The Tubs

The toilets in the mines were called "tubs." They were forty-five gallon drums that had been cut in two. There was lots of lime kept on hand to keep them sanitized. When they were full, they would be taken to the surface for disposal. The toilet area was basically a wooden frame with brattice hung over it to form a tent. There were 2x4 boards around the tubs that a man would stand on to use the facility. Clayton explains:

> Apparently they used to get a scattered feller, I don't know if it would be his birthday or something. You stood on the piece of plank, this 2 x 4, you just squat down. Going along the back, there'd be another board, just something to rest your back against. There were fellers would saw the plank so that the weight of yourself when you'd stand on it, you would plunk down. Now that's only stories I've been told. It never actually happened when I was around there.

Pit Clothes

They were that filthy, they used to stand up on their own.

The mine was commonly referred to as "the pit." Thus, work clothes and work boots were "pit clothes" and "pit boots." The iron ore was called "muck," and those who worked directly with extracting it were "muckers." This was an appropriate name because muck was exactly what the mixture of damp air and iron ore dust would form on the miners and their clothes. The clothes had to be able to withstand both the stress of accumulated layers of this muck and the harsh scrubbing required periodically to get the muck out. The type and amount of clothing worn by the Wabana miners was also determined by the fact that the temperature in the submarine slopes was always at least cool and sometimes freezing. According to Len:

> Going up on the submarine, everyone had to wear an overcoat summer and winter, because when you'd get on the trams, the further up you'd go, the colder it would get. And in the winter you'd have to put down your ear flaps, it would be that cold. Talk about cold. And the ice hanging down everywhere in the winter.

> But the mines was comfortable to work in because you never had no summer, you never had no winter, never no fall, never no spring. It was always the one temperature, about thirty-two degrees Fahrenheit. And you never found it cold. You'd wear Penman's underwear. Then you'd have heavy pants on, have the overalls with a bib and straps on top of that again. And you'd have your Penman's shirt. Then you'd have another fleece-lined shirt. Then you'd have a vest on top of that. And then you'd have the overall jacket over that.

The men who shovelled iron ore could not work for very long wearing the full rig-out of clothes. Once they started shovelling, they would strip off all the clothing down to the belt, including the inside shirt, because they would get so warm. George Picco says:

> Meself and Jack started to load, and we started to perspire. And we got that hot, we had to peel it all off. I tied me braces around me waist. Naked body!

Since it was damp and cold in the mines, as soon as they stopped loading, they would have to put all the clothing back on again while waiting for another empty car to come, because they would get cold very quickly.

Because of the nature of the work, drillers needed special clothing. Eric remembers:

> If you were working in a wet place, they would give you a pair of long rubbers and oil pants, but that was only on very rare occasions. On the last of it, drillers used to buy rubber clothes and they would last about twelve months. Oil clothes were no good because they would only last a few weeks, and they were two or three dollars a suit. They were made for fishing. The rubber was much better. You could scrape the dirt off it and, anyway, it did not take the dirt the way the cotton did.

Dry houses, where the men could change clothes and clean up after work, were located on the surface. When the men finished work, they would come up on the man trams. Some of them would go to the dry house and strip off. There was plenty of hot water there and big, white enamel pans:

> When you would come off shift, you had to wash in three different waters, but then the red dust would be in your nose, mouth, ears and throat.

There were ropes on pulleys going up to the ceiling above rows of seating. Each man had his own rope with a number on it. They would put their work clothes on hooks on these ropes and then hoist them up over the seats. Then they would get washed and put on their going-home clothes, cleaner overalls and a cleaner coat, that were kept in lockers there. When the men went back to work the next morning, the clothes left in the dry house would be warm and dry, ready to put on for another day's work.

Some men did not bother to go to the dry house to wash, but would walk home completely covered from hat to boots in iron ore dust. Their hands and faces and all would be one uniform dark red. It was a frightening sight for a young child, who probably would not recognize his own father covered in red dust. At home, they would wash themselves in the back porch or, on warm summer days, on the back bridge, or doorstep, and hang their work clothes in the porch for the next day. Some took off their outer work clothes and washed just their face and hands at the dry house, but that did not really do much good. When they got home, they would have to have a second wash:

> By the time you got home, your hands would be just as dirty again because the inside clothes would be as dirty as the coveralls that were taken off.

After a week, the iron ore dust on a miner's clothes would be "like hard icing, red and greasy." Drillers' work clothes would get particularly dirty because of the exhaust from the drill, so that sometimes the dirt would be a quarter of an inch thick. They were then brought home to be washed. The mainlandsmen carried their clothes around the bay in canvas bags or in cardboard boxes tied up with string. When they arrived home, they would leave the laundry outside the house because of bed bugs that infested the mess shacks.[72] Clayton says the coveralls would not be taken home to clean:

> You'd just wear them until they fell apart. I remember getting the pocket knife out and scraping the grease off to get another day or two out of them.

For many years there was no running water. The miner's wife had to bring the water from a well or pump and heat it in a large boiler on the wood and coal stove. She dissolved Gillette's Lye in this water, put in the clothes and swished them around with a wooden stick to loosen up the dirt. She then had the tricky task of lifting the clothes out with two wooden sticks and transferring them into a large galvanized tub. Then she poured water over the clothes to rinse the lye out so that her hands would not be burned by it during the washing. The lye was, nevertheless, still strong enough to cut the clothes, so it can be imagined what effect it had on her hands. She had to dump the rinse and wash waters outside the house because the iron ore residue would clog the drains. She did the wash "with her knuckles," using a scrubbing board and, most often, a bar of Sunlight soap. By this time the clothes would be "right slick and mucky." She used three changes of water, all of which had to be fetched and then dumped again. The clothes would be very heavy and stiff, making them difficult to scrub and wring out.

A suit of work clothes lasted three or four months. Eric, who had three suits of clothes at any one time, says proudly of his wife's washing ability, "I used to be the best-dressed man going in the mines."

Pit Boots

When Eric was very young, his father taught him how to make boots out of seal skin, how to sew a tap on them and how to take off the tap and sew an insole in the boot. Many miners learned this skill from their fathers and repaired their own boots as well as a cobbler could. Eric remembers getting a pair of boots in January that lasted him a full twelve months. He would put hob nails in them after he put the tap on, and they would last about six months. Then he would strip them right down and do them over again so that they would last for six more months. The men wore ordinary work boots until the 1950s, when wearing safety-toed boots became a requirement.

Hats

Hard hats were not worn until the later years of mining on Bell Island. Nobody wanted to wear them because they were so heavy. Then one day in 1950, a man was killed when a small rock fell down and hit him on the head. The doctor said that a hard hat would have saved his life. After that, the Company made it a rule that the men had to wear the hard hats. Up until that time, a soft canvas cap was worn. It had a little piece of leather on the front to clip the carbide lamp onto. The men lit the lamp and hooked it down over this piece of leather. These caps were purchased for about ninety-five cents at the Company store, which was located at the corner of Town Square and No. 2 Road. Gloves and safety glasses also became required items in later years.

Lamps

In the early years of the mining operation, the miner either used a candle or wore a little tin oil lamp, both of which attached to his cap. The lamp resembled a small teapot. It had a bib and a little cover on it and was stuffed tight with cotton waste. A piece of cotton was pulled out through the bib, and the lamp was filled with seal oil. When a man was shovelling or such work, he would set the lamp on something. But when he was teaming a horse, this lamp would be hooked into his cap, and the seal oil would run out and down over his face each time he bent over. Use of these lamps was discontinued around 1911. The lamp was a miniature version of lamps used by fishermen to light their fish stages and may have been adapted from that tradition.

The Scotia Company brought in the carbide lamp, which gave a better light and was used until the mid-1930s. The regular miner had a small one that could be hooked into his cap, but the foreman used a large one with a handle on it so that it could be hand-carried. The latter was called a high fidelity lamp. The men knew when the foreman was coming when they saw this much brighter light approaching.

Carbide resembled crushed stone and was about the size of peas. Each man would carry a can of it in his pocket. One can would be enough to last him all day. The carbide was put into a little container that was screwed up into the lamp. A small pocket on top of the lamp was filled with water. A little lever was turned which would allow a drop of water to drip down onto the carbide. A flint was used to light the resulting gas.

The carbide lamp was replaced by the electric lamp around 1935. For the electric lamp, each man would carry on his belt a seven and a half-pound storage battery connected by a cord which came up over his back to attach to the lamp in his cap. It was introduced for safety reasons because there had been some accidents caused by gas in the mines coming in contact with the carbide lamps. At first there had been no problem but, as the mines were extended further and further from the surface, trapped gas became more common, and some people were burned. The electric lamp did not give as good a light as the carbide, but still it was a better light to work with. For example, the carbide would often burn out and had to be relit. Eric can recall times when the flint was used out and he had no matches, so he would just continue drilling in the dark with no light whatsoever.

Brass

When a man was hired to shovel iron ore, he first went to the Company store, where he got a pit cap, a pit lamp, a can to fill with carbide and keep in his pocket to refill his lamp when necessary, and an iron ore shovel. Starting in 1925, he would also get a "brass." This was a round piece of brass, four centimeters in diameter. It had a number stamped on it that identified its owner, and from 1949 onward: "DOM. WABANA ORE LIMITED WABANA NFLD." It was placed in the check office, one of which was located at the entrance to each mine. When the men went into the mines, they had to go through this check office and past a wicket in single file, calling out their brass numbers as they did so. A man inside wrote down the numbers as they were called out. There were two big boards with finishing nails all over them and numbers below each nail. When a man was hired on, his brass was placed on one board. After the men had all gone down into the mines, the brasses with the numbers that had been called out were moved from one board to the other. In that way it was always known how many men were in the mines and who they were. Sometimes during the day, a timekeeper would go down into the mines and recheck to be sure. When the men came back up at the end of each shift, the operation was reversed.

Horses in the Mines

They were down there that long,
they knew where to go better than any man.

Before small engines were installed to do the job in the 1950s, horses were used in the mines to pull the empty ore cars to the face. They were large work horses, from 2,000 to 2,800 pounds and more, which were brought from Nova Scotia and kept in barns down in the mines. "After months in the mines, when they would be taken to the surface, they would be unable to see for days." Len recalls:

> We had fourteen down in No. 3, big horses. We had one over in No. 6 was down there twenty-six years. She was thirty year old when they brought her up. She was called Blind Eye Dick. She had one eye, you see,

so we called her Blind Eye Dick. And she was down in the mines twenty-six years. And they brought her up and retired her. They put her in this big field up by Scotia barn. And when she come to herself, she was just like a young colt going around, and she bawling. She was worth looking at. And she was about a ton, 2,000 pounds, the biggest kind of a horse. There was some beautiful horses down in the mines. They used to come from Nova Scotia. They pulled the empty cars in to the loaders, the men to load. Albert Miller was down in No. 3 Mines, that's who was looking after the horses down there. Mr. French was up in No. 4 Mines. Andrews was down in No. 3 barn. Anderson Carter, he was down in No. 1 barn. The fellers that were teamsters, that would be their job. Well, if you had a horse, well you'd look after it. You'd go down, when you'd bring her in, probably two o'clock or half past two or three o'clock, you'd take your brush and put her in the stall, haul the collar off her. That's all they'd have on was the collar. Take the collar off and the reins, hang them up. You'd take your brush and brush her all down and comb her down and everything else, till she'd be shining. And then you'd go over to the bin and take about two gallons of oats and throw in to her. And take a block of hay and throw that in her stall and break it up for her.

Eric remembers that, when he was a boy working in the mines, he and his friends used to have "a pretty good time riding horseback coming out over the levels and driving the horses when there was nobody watching."

George recalls his first experience working with a horse in the mines. He had been working underground for only a short time and was not familiar with the slopes. One day he was asked to "go teaming" because one of the men who usually did that job was off sick:

> Skipper Dick Walsh said, "Were you ever teaming?" I said, "No, sir." He said, "You were never teaming?" Now this is taking a horse out of a barn and going in wherever you had to go with the horse and pull empty boxes (ore cars) in to the face of the room to the hand-loaders. I said, "No, sir, I was never teaming." "Well," he said, "Ern Luffman is off now today, and there's nobody to take the horse out of the barn to go in where you'll be working. You'll have to go in and take his horse out and go in west." "Well, sir," I said, "I don't know me way in west." He said, "You needn't to worry about that. The horse will take you right where you got to go." I said, "I hope you're right, sir." He said, "I know I'm right. Don't have any fear if you don't know where to go. The horse will take you there." I said, "Okay, sir. I'll go in, and I'll take the horse out of the barn."

> Bloody big red mare. I went in the barn and got the horse out of the barn, and I held the reins behind him and he started off. I didn't know where to go. And he kept on going and going. And by and by he made a turn, and he got out in the middle of the track and he went, kept on going and going and going. By and by he turned off the track, and he went this way and he brought up against a big door, enormous big door, and he stopped. I went and I sized up the door. There was a big handle on it. I takes hold of the door and pulls it open, and he went on in through. Not a light, no lights. And he waited for me, and I closed the door. I got the reins and I walked behind him, and he kept on going and going and going. By and by he comes to

another bloody big door. He stopped and I had to open that and, after I opened it, he went through the door. And I closed it and I took hold of the reins, and he went on again. I was tired, not knowing when he'd get there. He was taking me. I wasn't taking him.

And he kept on going, going, going, and by and by I thought I see a light. I said, "That's a light, if I knows anything." A little sparkle of light about that size. You're a hell of a way from it then, see, looking right ahead in the dark. And the horse kept on going and going and going. And by and by the light started to get bigger, and the horse kept on going. And he brought me right into the headway. Now the headway was where the trips of ore used to be running up and down on a slant. And he passed over the tracks and he went on. I still had the reins in my hand. He kept on going and going and going, and by and by he made a turn, kept on going down the grade, and by and by he makes another turn, going in this way. And here I sees two lights way into the face in the room. And, as Skipper Dick Walsh said it, he said, "He'll take you right where you got to go."

And he went on in this room and right where Ern Luffman took the swing off of him [the day before] – the swing was two ropes on either side of the horse and a bar here and a hook where you used to hook into the cars – this is where he come. He come and stood right by the swing. And the two hand-loaders got up and put the swing on him, and I had to go right out on the landing and hook the swing into two cars, and the horse hauled them right into the two men and they loaded 'em up. Well, that was my job for that day. As they had the first two cars there loaded, they took them out on the landing, and I had to go out with the horse again, hook two more and haul them in until they got their twenty boxes loaded. Then I had to take the horse back to the barn again. But you couldn't fool a horse in the mines. Yes sir, they really knew their way around.[73]

Rats in the Mines

The rats were thousands.

The miners' other "companions," that also "really knew their way around," were the rats. Some of them were a foot long, "big as cats." In fact, Eric says, the rats thrived in the mines because of the horses, eating the bran and oats that were brought down to feed them:

> While the horses were down there, there was no chance of them being hungry because they'd live around the stables, you see. They'd get in the oat boxes.

The oats were stored in large molasses puncheons, the insides of which were very smooth. Sometimes they would be covered but, at any rate, it was rare for the rats to be able to get into them. One time the mines were shut down for a couple of months, and some rats managed to get into a puncheon to get the remaining oats. Then they could not get out again because the inside was so smooth. Harold saw one of these puncheons half full of rats that had eaten out all the oats and then had started eating each other.

Another source of food for the rats was the scraps from the miners' lunches. When it was dinner time, George says, the rats would come around and "they wouldn't knock at the doors either." One man said that when he was eating a piece of bread, he would eat down to the part that he was holding in his ore-coated hand and then throw the remainder to the rats. There was usually a rat there to run and get it. If there were no rats around, he would throw it in the garbage can. They'd get in there and get it anyway. Albert says:

> They'd almost tell you when it was mug-up time. You couldn't lay your lunch down on a bench, or anything like that.

Eric tells how the dry houses were set up to take account of the rats:

> They used to serve your lunch room barbarous, you know. You had to have a string right up on the ceiling tied right along on a wire, tie your lunch on the wire. They'd even get out there and cut off the lunches and let them drop down when they were real hungry.

While the rats were not as numerous by the time Clayton started working, there were still lots of them around. They were most noticeable just after the annual vacation, when the mines had been closed down for two weeks. They would be really hungry then:

> There was a lot of electrical equipment, huge motors. What we'd do, the last shift that you'd work, you'd put 200 watt bulbs on these motors. Now there'd be wires running everywhere because you'd have to put the wires around the motors to create a bit of heat to keep the dampness away. If you didn't, it would ruin the motors within two weeks because there was a lot of dampness. Now before the mines started up on a Monday, there'd be a crew go down and lots of times I was elected to go down, and we'd go down on a Saturday to take all these wires away and get everything ready for operation. So you'd sit around

for your lunch and just stay quiet and they'd come around. I'm not exaggerating, there'd be a couple of hundred. I've seen them open a lunch can. Now that is the truth as I'm sitting here. So what we used to do, in the lunch can where the haspes go up, there was little holes. And we'd get what you call a bronze welding rod and you'd make a clip and you'd put through [the holes so the rats couldn't open them]. And that was the reason for that. Once the mines would get started up for a week or two, they wouldn't come around like that then.

Some miners killed rats whenever the opportunity arose, kicking them with their boots or hitting them on the head with a rock. Others would not think of hurting them:

> No old miners would kill a rat. But young miners used to do this and the old guys said that if you killed a rat, the rest of 'em would come along and eat your lunch and clothes up and so on. They were fooling, but that's what they thought, those old guys.[74]

Eric remembers:

> I never killed one in my life. But I've seen fellers that if they saw them, they had to catch them. One feller, if he'd see a rat, he'd shift a pile of rock from here over to that door to get the rat out. Had to catch him. But I never did. Never killed one in my life.

Other miners were oblivious to the rats, while still others treated them like pets. Albert says that the rats were company. He did not mind them. When he was working on the hoist, he tamed a couple of young ones. He would throw crumbs to them and they would come up to his feet.

Rats were common in the mines for a long time but were

practically cleaned out in later years. This was partly due to the modernization program in the early 1950s which saw the horses replaced by small engines. As well, Albert recalls a concerted effort to clean up the mines:

> You'd hardly see a rat down there when the mines closed down. I think it started when Mr. Dickey went manager over there.[75] He started to clean out the mines and the garbage. Everything used to be taken up. And they dropped stuff down to get rid of them. When the mines went down, I don't think there was hardly a rat down there in No. 3.

Some Wabana miners believed that seeing rats leaving a mine meant something was going to happen. Others believed more specifically that it meant flooding.[76]

Harold recalls experiences he had with rats:

> There was a rheostat, a heater from the engine that used to use up the electricity. It had an iron top on it which would get very warm. It was a nice place to lie down for a nap.

He would lie down on it sometimes during his break, but there was not always a lot of comfort. "The rats would be there in the dark but, as long as you kicked the iron every now and then, they would stay away." If he fell asleep, when he awoke there was sure to be a rat on his leg.

While Albert says that he tamed rats to come up to his feet when he was working on the hoist, Eric tells a bizarre tale of another man who also tamed a rat while working on the main hoist:

> In those times, the hoist was boarded right in. It was a pretty warm place because there was no ventilation in

there. Georgie had this rat, oh, a big rat. He told us it took months and months to get that rat to come and eat. The rat would eat the food he'd fire to him. But he wouldn't come handy to him. Georgie knew the rat. Matter of fact, he had the rat branded with a piece of copper wire, G. P. marked on it. The rat ran away and didn't come back for days after that happened. But he edged his way back and anyone who'd go in, the rat would disappear. And nobody believed Georgie. Some of the boys then began to sneak around and they saw the rat sure enough. Now Georgie had a bench to lie on with a piece of brattice filled up with grass for a pillow. When there was no cars running, Georgie would lie down and go to sleep. You could do that before in the iron mines. And the rat used to lie down on the pillow and have a nap. Georgie was telling about the rat now every day, and telling his sister to put a little bit of extra bread in for the rat. He was living with his sister. He thought the world of the rat. He used to wash the rat, look after him, clean him up. The rat loved him. This is what Georgie was telling the other fellers that worked around there. There was no doubt about the rat, because Dick Brien, the boss, walked in this day and there was the rat, laid down on the couch, on the cushion. And the minute he saw him, he was gone. So there was no doubt about the rat. After a long time, a good many fellers now saw the rat. This day Georgie started the motor and the rat ran and this is where he went, right into this motor. And Georgie didn't know that he was there. By and by he smelled him, and he stopped the motor and there was the rat. Georgie wouldn't work there after that. They had to give him a change. He thought the world of the bloody rat.

One day, when some miners were in a particularly idle mood, they caught a rat and connected its hind leg and tail to the terminals of a blasting battery. They then let the rat run into a puddle of water to ground it out, then they pulled the battery: "All you could see were sparks." Clayton recalls:

> There were fellers who would get them and put them in an old drill hole, one that never blasted off. They would probably be in eight or twelve, some of them twenty feet. They'd put the rat in and the rat would go in, you'd stuff him in the hole. Some fellers would put a glove on, more fellers just wouldn't care. But anyway, they'd get an extra large one and they'd stuff him into the hole, now this is head on now, and you'd wait and you'd wait and you'd wait and you'd wait, and he'd come out head on every time. Oh, I've seen fellers sticking the rat's head in their mouth. I don't know if they were showing off. I didn't get no sense in why a person would want to do that.

Apparently, when the opportunity presented itself, rats were not the only creatures that could be used to help ease the tedium of work. Some miners caught a buck goat once and hauled oil pants on over his front legs and an oil coat over his hind legs. They stuck an old cap on his head and put an old carbide lamp on him and let the goat go. A similar incident was reported in *The Daily News* in 1912:

> There was considerable amusement around the mines one day when a Billy Goat was seen leading a herd of goats attired in a sou'wester and a pair of ladies corsets secured around him, with his horns out through the top and the strings tied under his chin.[77]

SIX

SKYLARKING

You wouldn't be fired, you'd be hung.

Harold Kitchen

WE HAVE ALREADY seen how several miners obtained work with the Company at Wabana. Here are two humorous stories describing how some men from Upper Island Cove appealed for work:

> When Leander Hussey of Island Cove first went to Bell Island to get a job, he was asked if he had a preference as to which mine he wanted to work in: No. 2, 3 or 4. Hussey replied, "I don't care if you puts me in Primer, so long as it's a job."

> Another Island Cove man who was looking for a job went to see the manager, Mr. McDonald, who told him, "We're filled right up and can't take anyone else on." Not to be deterred, the man quipped, "Well, would you take me on and bust?"[78]

One man describes how, after being hired on, he was introduced to his new co-workers:

You were always introduced to the others as, "So and so's oldest son. Now that's so and so, married to such and such from the eastern end of the Island." Your whole history was told before you uttered a word to them. One thing that stands out was that you were always recognized as your father's son instead of by your own Christian name.[79]

After the introductions, it was common for someone to play an initiation prank on the newcomer, often sending him to look for nonexistent tools, materials, or other items. Clayton recalls:

When I went underground, they sent me off one time looking for a skyhook. I didn't know then, but it was an old trick, and they got a laugh out of it. I went to the warehouse and I said I was sent for a skyhook. And, of course, they got a great laugh out of it. I was a bit shy at the time and took it to heart.

Ron recalls his own initiation:

Oh, they played tricks on you. Oh yes, they did. Like, they told me the first day on the job, to go down and get something. I forget what it was but it was perfectly ridiculous. And I, because I wanted to please, was half in a turn, with a foot half down to go in the direction, when I realized that this fella was pulling my leg, and I turned back and laughed, you know. Everybody laughed and that was it. But, no, part of your initiation was that, go down and get a wheelbarrow full of smoke or, you know, go down and fill this up with air, you know, get a bottle of mist down by the dam.

He also remembers when his foreman tried to pull an old initiation prank on a boy from Upper Island Cove. The Island

Cove men were renowned on Bell Island for their ability to get the better of the bosses, and the boy in this narrative, young though he probably was, proved himself a worthy member of that community:

> John Charles Vokey said to this little Island Cove fella, "Now, you're starting work, and I want you to go down and get me a wheelbarrow full of smoke." And the little Island Cover said to him, "All right, Cock. You load it and I'll bring it up."

Here is another story about a young fellow who was nobody's fool:

> When the No. 6 deckhead was being built, the foreman decided to have some sport with the nipper boy, so he ordered him to go get a round square. The boy was given no explanation or description of what this round square was supposed to be. Off he went to the home of Mrs. Nolan, a lady who made and sold spruce beer, and returned a short time later with a dozen bottles of the stuff. As he handed them around to his fellow workers, he said to the boss, "Here's your *round*, sir, and you can *square* it at Mrs. Nolan's later."[80]

Eric does not recall being sent on any fool's errands, but he does remember being "baptized with piss." He was in the mines working with three men one day when one of them jumped up on a barrel. The man grabbed a piece of brattice that was covering an air vent and wrapped it around himself like a priest's robe. In mock-solemn voice he pronounced, "I baptize thee Narrow Gauge, in the name of the Father and of the Son and of the Holy Ghost." Then he proceeded to urinate on young Eric's head.

George remembers his first day underground vividly, for the

experience was completely different from anything that had gone before in his life. His first job had been on the surface, but it was seasonal work, and he was laid off each winter when shipping ended. He and a buddy decided they wanted to work year round, so they went to see Billy Tucker, the man who did the hiring, to see if they could get a job underground. There were many different jobs in the mines, but the one that an unskilled man would be most likely to start out doing was shovelling iron ore. Mr. Tucker told them that this was the only job available and that they both seemed too slight of build for such work. George's reply was, "Slight or slight not, I wants to get down in the mines." They were given the jobs, but were cautioned that they had to "get twenty boxes a day," that is, they had to load twenty ore cars between the two of them. Each car held one and three-quarter tons, so that each man was expected to hand-load seventeen and a half tons of iron ore a day.

The next day they went to the Company store and got their pit caps, lamps and iron ore shovels, and headed down into No. 2 Mine. This was George's first time ever underneath the collar, the entrance to the mine. When they got off the man trams in the main slope, half the men went east and half went west, all going in different directions to their particular jobs. Skipper Billy Reader, who was foreman down in the tunnel, addressed George and his buddy:

> "All right, you two strange fellers," he said, "come on with me." We had the iron ore shovels on our shoulders, and we followed Skipper Billy Reader. And he opened up a big door and, gentle God, the steam come out. You couldn't see hardly anything. "My Christ, Jack," I said, "where in the hell are we going to go?" "Come on," [Reader] said, "come on with me."

The stairway going down was very steep and seemed to be about seventy-five or eighty feet long. They came to a level and then went down another flight which was equally long, so that they thought they were never going to be able to get back up out of it:

> Anyway, we followed Skipper Billy Reader into the face, into the room. By and by he stopped. And here was the big pile of iron ore right into the face. "Now," he said, "get your twenty here today. We wants twenty boxes."

There were horses and teamsters there, hauling in boxes (ore cars) to the hand-loaders. One of them pulled in a box for George and Jack. They were given a sprag each. This was a piece of round iron about two feet long that was shoved into the wheel so the car would not roll away:

> Meself and Jack started to load the iron ore car. Anyway, we started to perspire. And we got that warm and hot, be golly, we had to peel it all off. I tied me braces around me waist. Naked body! I don't think we loaded our twenty that day. We loaded eighteen. Anyway, to make a long story short, all that week meself and Jack, we kept loading iron ore. Saturday, we used to work Saturdays and all, Saturday, when we had our last car loaded with iron ore, Jack he looked at me, and he took the shovel that way, held it over his head, and he said, "George, there's better ways than this to try and make a living. Now," he said, "this finishes me." And he took the shovel and let it go up by the rib and he said, "shovel, bye-bye." The two of us went out to the main slope and waited for the trams to go up on, and we went up on deck and Jack never went underneath the collar after.

Mining was hard, serious work, so it is no wonder that boys and men alike, both above and below ground, engaged in skylarking, or horseplay, to relieve the tension whenever the opportunity presented itself. One of Eric's early memories is of an incident of unpremeditated vandalism which almost got him, and the group of boys with whom he worked, fired. A lot of these boys were twelve and thirteen year old orphans who had come to work on Bell Island from various places around Conception Bay. Their fathers were among 173 crewmen lost when their sealing ship, the *Southern Cross*, mysteriously disappeared in early April 1914. The foremen treated these boys the same as they would treat their own sons.

Eric's foreman was Richard Brien of Topsail. Brien had a boat at the pier, and he and the men on his crew used to row home across the Tickle every Saturday evening after work. Naturally they were eager to get away as soon after work as possible, leaving the boys who stayed on Bell Island to finish up. They were working on an electric shovel at the time of this incident. When the shift finished on Saturday afternoon and the shovel came off the tracks, the boys would make everything safe before getting on the trams to come up on deck. There were nine or ten of them in the group.

The slope was all lit up with white and green lights in the bays for safety and red lights where the cars used to pass. As they rode up in the man trams on this occasion, one of the boys idly began taking pot shots at the lights, using small rocks that had accumulated on the floor of the tram. Soon all the boys joined in the fun, and the upshot was that they broke all the lights in the slope. On Sunday, Eric was summoned from home to go to the office to see Mr. McLean, the boss man with the Scotia Company in those early years. McLean told him that he had had men working all morning replacing the broken bulbs:

He was a big man. He said to me, "Eric, I could fire all ye fellers and that wouldn't do ye any harm because ye'd love it. But your mothers would pay for it. I'm not going to fire you, but I'll tell you this, just like I'd do to me own son, I'm going to do to you. Take down your pants and lean across that chair there." First I was going to say no. Then I thought about what he said about losing my job and so forth. I thought he was joking. He was a big man, and he had a big belt about three inches wide, for buckling over a big old coat he used to put on for coming up [the slope] on the car where it was so cold, his fur-lined coat. So anyway, I finally decided I'd take the crack. I leaned across the chair and he gave me a crack. Well, first I thought I might cry, and I couldn't do that. But the tears began to come out, and I knew I wasn't going to sit down for a while, not in comfort. "Now," he said, "don't you speak of this to nobody. Now get out of here."

I went out a little ways and I met Jim Harvey going in. "How did you get on?" he said. Now Jimmie George was after being in and telling Jim what time to come. "Best kind," I said. "I'm going to work again tomorrow morning." There was a lot of woods, timber woods around there then where it wasn't cut out at that time and some grassy spots in among it. So I got in there and I lay down in the shade, and I waited until Harvey come out. Well, he got up along side of me and he began to curse on me blue murder, [wanting to know] why didn't I tell him. And we see Jimmie Pike going in. We don't say nothing. Wasn't very long before he come out. Anyway, I suppose there was Heber Anthony and, anyhow, the last feller went in, his name was Parsons, Georgie Parsons. He was fifteen years old. He was well developed. He could put a man three hundred pounds over his head. I seen him do it. He was a bit of a fighter. Nice feller.

So when he went in, the old man said to him, Mr. McLean said, "Parsons," now [Georgie] was the one driving the shovel, see, "what happened to you?" Now he knew nothing at all about what was taking place, that there was fellers moaning up in the woods. He knew nothing about this. He said, "Mr. McLean, I'm responsible for everything that happened." He said, "I was the driver of the shovel. I'm the man that Mr. Brien left in charge. I'm awfully sorry the thing had to go the way it did, but that's how it is. I was just as bad as any of them, and I should have had better sense." He was perhaps fifteen or sixteen years old. He come from the Labrador that year anyhow. "Parsons," Mr. McLean said, "I got a proposition to make to you. Every feller that came in here, see that belt there, leaned across the chair there and I belted him. And some of them are going to have a problem sitting for a while. I done that to remind you fellers that when you're sitting down, you're not supposed to throw rocks. Now if you're satisfied to take that the same as the other fellers, Parsons, fine. If not, I got your time wrote out here. You can get your money and quit." Now if Parsons didn't want to let him do it, he wouldn't have been able to do it because, as I said before, he was as tough as anyone. He said, "Mr. McLean, whatever you give them young fellers, you give me twice as much."

Now we all decided that perhaps it was best not to talk about it at all to nobody. First we were ashamed to think that we were humiliated to such an extent. And I don't suppose anybody ever told that story after, because we were ashamed, see. But we didn't have too much choice. It was that or be hungry, because things weren't so good as they are now. Anyway, we went back to work the next morning. But my mother had to get a cushion for me to sit on for three or four days.

Albert recalls that there was always a lot of fun of a childish kind going on with the boys on the picking belt:

> There was a bunch of us young fellers. I was only sixteen then. We'd be carrying on. We'd play tricks on each other and on the boss, too. I remember our boss on the picking belt, Mr. Davis, he had a big mustache. And I sneaked down behind him one day and I held onto this mustache and I kept holding on. I was afraid to let him go. I finally let him go, and I had to take off. He throwed the rocks at me. He was pretty good, you know. He was a little bit good on that stuff himself. He played tricks, too, on the boys. As long as you done your work, he was okay. If you never done your work, he'd get mad. The most kind of things he used to do to the boys was call you names, and then you'd do something to him. He wouldn't do very much playing tricks or anything cause he was a real old man.

In the following narrative, Harold recalls how a group of boys played an old practical joke on a boss. The belt-house door consisted of a large door with a smaller door cut out of it:

> The smaller one was used most of the time. When you came in through that door at the bottom of No. 2 belt-house, you had to stoop to get in through. One old chap, Tom Craig from the West Mines, was boss over the samplers. This day when he came in, the boys had a bucket of water rigged up over the door. When he came in the door, he stooped to get in and the water all poured down the back of his neck.

Lunch was a popular time for playing a practical joke on someone. It was a break from work when there was no danger of being reprimanded for goofing off. There were also lots of props handy that made prank-playing easy. When Harold was younger, one of his jobs was heating water for lunch time. He and the other boys used to have a lot of fun heaving water at one another:

> You would get a can of water and hide behind a corner. When another feller would come around the corner, you would give it to him in the mouth.

Sometimes he had to go to the home of one or another of the men to get a forgotten lunch so that, when the man saw him coming with a paper bag in his hand, he would be expecting to have his lunch passed to him. Harold would play a trick by filling up a paper bag with water and then putting it into another bag. When he would get up close to the fellow, he would hit him in the side of the face with the bag:

> It would burst and the guy would be drowned with water. That was an old trick and you could only get away with it a few times.

One day Harold was the butt of a prank. When he went to get his lunch can from the cupboard, he could not budge it. On examining it, he found that someone had taken out his lunch, driven a four-inch nail down through the can and on through the shelf, buckled the nail under the bottom of the shelf and put the lunch back into the can. Clayton used a similar trick to "get back" at the men who played the initiation prank on him. He would usually wait until they had eaten their lunch. When they would go down to hand in their shift, he would nail the lunch box to the table. When the victim would come back and grab his lunch box by the handle, the top part would come off in his hand and the bottom would stay nailed to the table. Clayton would also nail coats onto the wall.

It often happened, though, that what started out as a bit of fun would end in a row. This happened on one occasion when a prankster took advantage of a religious observance to play a prank. The miners generally respected each other's religious beliefs, one of which was that devout Roman Catholics and Anglicans alike would not eat meat on Fridays:

> The Catholic people, they wouldn't eat meat on Friday. No odds if they starved to death, they wouldn't eat meat on Friday. And there was one feller worked with us, Uncle John Fitzpatrick. And one day a feller by the name of Dinn Sheehan from Harbour Grace, he was a devil for carrying on, one day he went over in the old cupboard, and he found this great big chunk of salt beef. And he said to Uncle John Fitzpatrick, he said, "Would you like to have a piece of salt meat?" "Yes, Dinn boy," he said. So Dinn takes it out of the cupboard and lays it on Uncle John's lunch paper. We used to have lunch in a paper, you know. And he took the piece of salt meat up, not knowing anything, you know. And he had about two bites took out of it, and he said, "God damn you, Sheehan, this is Friday." Then he chased Sheehan with the piece of meat.

There were also times when the men had some free time while still on the job. When the work was held up while the face cleaners removed loose rock after a blast, or while the shovellers were waiting for empty cars to load, they were said to be "delayed in the day." These delays were passed in various ways. Usually the men simply "took a spell" and smoked a cigarette. It was a chance for them to chat and exchange gossip or stories. They also tossed horseshoes on the level or played checkers in the dry house. Checkers appear metaphorically in one humorous narrative:

> Two Island Cove men were working down in a huge opening when one of them noticed that the foreman had been staring at them for a long period of time. One of the men said, "Say, Skipper, can you play checkers?" "Yes," replied the foreman, "why?" "Because if you don't move, you're gonna lose two men."[81]

As might be expected, idle time like this was ripe for a little horseplay, which sometimes took the form of a sham fight. Two men would be chosen to fight, and all the others would make bets of a few cents each on who would win. One day the men persuaded their overman, who was a very serious man, to be the referee. Everything was going well until one of the fighters struck one of the observers. When the overman/referee tried to break it up, he got pushed around, and the whole crew ended up in a free-for-all.

Another time, one miner took advantage of another's physical pain to play a practical joke on him. The victim was known as a "comical stick" and had "queer old sayings." Perhaps, because of these traits of his personality, it was felt that he could take a joke, and this may have been why this grotesque prank was played on him. He was complaining of a toothache, so one of the boss men told him that a certain miner could charm teeth. Unknown to him, the charmer went to the tubs and hooked up some faeces on a stick. He put a bit on his finger and then went and told the man, as charmers usually do, that he was going to charm his tooth, but that he should not tell anyone that he had done it. He told him that after he put his finger on the tooth, the man should keep his mouth closed for a while. So he stealthily put the faeces on the tooth, and the suffering man closed his mouth. Of course, he realized immediately that he had been duped and, "if he hadda caught him after, he would have made away with him."

Eric remembers a man who found himself at work one day without his cigarettes, a situation which put him in mental anguish until he was given a substitute by a more than helpful fellow worker:

Neddie used to drive the stock pile hoist. He used to pull the car up to the stock pile, shut off the engine when she dumped and lower her back. If it went too far, it would go over. Anytime he was off work, we were sure to have a stock pile car off the road. This morning he came to work and he had no cigarettes. He thought she was going to go over if he didn't have a cigarette. The cable man was in the shed. He knew all about ropes and cables. He took a piece of manila rope, chopped it up in small pieces and rolled it up in cigarette paper. "Here," he said, "try that." Well, Neddie got so gay, and from that day on he smoked it.

The rules got stiffer in later years and anyone caught playing practical jokes or engaging in horseplay could get suspended. This seems to have been a result of tighter control by management, combined with the more delineated regulations for behaviour that came with the presence of the Union. Harold emphasized the change over the years by saying, "If you did some of these things in later years, you wouldn't be fired, you'd be hung."

SEVEN

Mishaps, Ghosts and Fairies

A miner's life is a hard life, buried alive every day.

George Picco

THE WABANA MINES were relatively safe and comfortable when
compared to other mining operations, yet fatalities occurred
with amazing regularity. Approximately one hundred men
lost their lives in various mining accidents over the lifetime of
the mines and countless others were injured. The miners say
that they never worried about the danger involved in their
work. The narratives they relate about mining accidents
indicate that they probably were always unconsciously aware of
it though. The fun they sought to inject into their work lives
was undoubtedly their way of balancing conditions that, while
not oppressive, were far from ideal.

There were no major disasters in the Bell Island mines: "two
or three men trapped was the usual thing." A methane gas
explosion in No. 6 Mine in 1938, in which two men died and
another seven were injured, was one of the worst. The mine
had been closed for a time and was being reopened again when
this happened. George Picco remembers it this way:

An inspection was being made of the rooms to see if they were safe for the men to work in. Eight or nine men went into a room, and one man took out a match to light a cigarette. They were blown to pieces. A lot of men got burned. Work had to be shut down. Stretchers were gotten and a lot of men were brought out to the main slope. Their clothes had caught fire. They were just about burned to death. A lot of them lost their noses and their ears. They had to be rushed over to St. John's. Some of them died. That was the first time that ever happened.

Eric Luffman comments on the same explosion:

It killed Sam Chaytor and Bobby Bowdring. Bobby's son Frank was maimed, and another feller, Charlie Skanes. The other five weren't so badly burned. That explosion was caused by methane gas. What happened there was the place was loaded with gas and a feller went to light his pipe.

An accident could happen at any time, taking the life of a buddy or friend without any warning:

I remember my next-door neighbour was walking up the mine one day, getting off work. And had his head bent some to help pick his steps, when a piece of ore, no bigger than a fist, fell and hit him on the head. Killed him. So you see, sometimes it didn't matter how careful you were.[82]

There is great pain when a co-worker is killed, but pangs of regret linger on when a man believes that a simple action on his part might have saved his friend's life:

You'd always hear stories from men who were working with men who died alongside them, had an accident, or were killed. There was a man I knew well and I was talking to him, and five minutes after, he was killed. If I hadda stayed with him a little bit longer, maybe he wouldn't. He went off cleaning down the side of a rib, you know. A piece of ground came down and hit him on the head. If I hadda stayed there talking to him, he wouldn't have been doing that, because it wasn't his job. I left talking to him and I just went out over the level and down the headway. And I was talking to the boss, Leo Brien his name was, and while I was talking to him, a feller came running down the headway singing out for the stretcher. This man was after getting hit. He wasn't killed right out. He died on the way up.

It was tragedy enough just hearing that a friend was killed, but often the men had to bear the pain of being witness at the scene of the accident:

Once when I reported for work on the four o'clock shift, I had to go down the mine where a man had just been killed and shut off the air valve. I'll never forget the sight of him. His head was nearly blown off, and several men had to strap him to a stretcher to hold him until he died. It didn't take long.[83]

Harold Kitchen recalls the 1952 accident in which a man was run over by the large twenty-ton car. "He was killed by the big car that ran back and forth in No. 3 Mine." It was believed he was there four hours, with the car running over him every eight minutes:

The trams, with way over two hundred men coming off shift around 12:20 a.m., did not see the accident, because at this point the water was leaking from the roof and everybody turned their backs in the opposite direction, sometimes pulling the collar of their coats over their heads. So at around 12:45 a.m., we got on the trams to go back in the mines on the back shift. Just as we got at this point, the trams stopped and the first I knew, Jack Barrett, who was supervisor on this shift, jumped off and he shouted, "Boys, we have an accident here and a bad one." Some men ran up the slope. Others got sick and scared. Jack Barrett was the man who ran back to the office and notified those in authority.

The body was cut up in hundreds of pieces at this time. Somebody arrived with the stretcher. An older man by the name of William Janes, the blaster foreman who was noted for seeing bad accidents, was right alongside of me when the trams stopped. Very few other men handled the body. Some men stayed but could not touch anything. Billy Janes used to pick up parts in both hands and put them on the stretcher with the main body, as it was scattered a long way. I used to work part time on the ambulance and at undertaker's work, so I was used to it. When we got him to the collar, the ambulance was waiting. So a fellow by the name of Ben Burke got in the ambulance with me, plus the driver, Bert Rideout, and we took the remains to the Company fire hall. They made an iron box at the machine shop and brought it to the fire hall. So there, Bert Rideout and myself, with dozens of witnesses standing around, placed the remains in the box and took it back to the machine shop and had the cover welded on. And then the iron box was placed in a casket. This man was a very large man, about 220 pounds, and a very nice man. He was a supervisor with a company from Ontario.

A retirement party held at the Union Hall of Local 4121 of the United Steel Workers of America in 1957. Sitting (left to right): Leo McCarthy, Sam Bickford, Walt Bickford, Edmund Head, John Power(?), Harry Hammond, (captain of No. 4 Mine), Jack Harvey (blasting foreman of No. 4 Slope, who was retiring after 44 years service), Roy Paddon (superintendent of No. 4), Edward Bickford, Mike Hickey. Standing (left to right): Warren Parsons, Tom McDonald, Billy Dobbin, Ray Gosse, unidentified.

David Ignatius "Nish" Jackman, who was president of the Wabana Mine Workers' Union from 1941 to 1964. (He was ousted for a brief period between 1956 to 1958.) A colourful character who stood tough for the miners' rights, he captured the hearts and imaginations of Bell Islanders and negotiated many benefits while averting major strikes.

Courtesy of Eric Luffman

This picture was probably taken in the 1940s. Eric Luffman (left) became mine captain of No. 3 in 1946. When he finished with the company in 1967, he had 51 years of service. Thomas (Tommy) J. Gray (centre) was mine superintendent of No. 3. He had worked in the coal mines of Nova Scotia before coming to Bell Island around 1920 as a ventilation expert. He died in 1954. Fred J. Newton (right) was overman of No. 3 Slope when he retired in 1956 after 46 years of service.

Courtesy of the Provincial Archives, The Rooms Corporation of Newfoundland and Labrador

The DOSCO-owned ore-carrier, S.S. Wabana, *making ready to load at Scotia Pier. The* Wabana *was engaged in the ore trade between Bell Island and Sydney, Nova Scotia, when this picture was taken in 1955 and, at that time, held the fastest loading record at Scotia Pier – 9,500 tons in one hour, thirty-two minutes. (*Submarine Miner 3 *(12): 4 December 1956).*

Ship loading iron ore at Scotia Pier. In the left of the photo is the "cage" used for getting up and down the steep cliff. The stockpiling area was above the pier. The Dominion Pier was further along the shore to the right (between the Scotia Pier and the Beach). The loading conveyors were a system of endless buckets extending from the loading tower at the pier head to a point underneath the ore-product stored in the loading bins by the stacker conveyor. The ore-loading chutes at the top of the loading tower would be lowered and ore cargo, moved from the bins by the loading conveyor, would pour into the waiting holds of the freighter at the rate of 120 tons per minute.

Gerald Parsons operates a Joy Loader at No. 3 Slope in 1956. These machines were used exclusively in No. 3 and replaced men who had shovelled muck by hand. The machine was 25 feet long by 6 1/2 feet wide by 5 1/2 feet high and weighed 19 tons. It was electrically operated. Traction and loading were powered by a 75-hp motor. Two 15-hp motors supplied power for conveying the ore from the rotary gathering arms to the far end of the loading boom. At this point, the ore was transferred to a 35-foot shuttle car, which was brought up behind the machine. This in turn transported the product to four-ton ore cars. The loading unit was manned by a crew of four: a loader operator and helper; and two shuttle car operators. (Submarine Miner 3 (9): 2 Sept. 1956) The spray from the hose kept down the dust and facilitated the flow of ore on the conveyor.

131

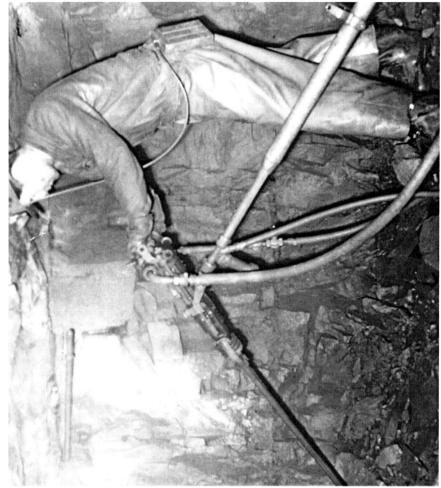

Vince Dalton, wearing rubber clothes and a battery pack to power his lamp, operates a J-40 jack-leg air-compressed drill, c. 1956. The average ore face was 24 feet wide and from 9 to 14 feet high. Arranged in 3 horizontal rows of 8, 24 holes were bored into the face ranging from 7 to 10 feet in depth and spaced at 2-foot intervals. Holes were slanted to form a wedge in the centre. When the face was blasted by delayed action, the centre was first blown free, providing space for the remaining ore to break clear. From 200 to 500 tons of well-broken ore was usually the result. (Submarine Miner 3 (11): 7, Nov. 1956)

The scene at the entrance to No. 3 Mine as one group of men finishes their shift and another prepares to board the man rake to begin their two and one-quarter mile journey down the Main Slope, c. 1954.

At the left of this c. 1958 photo, the No. 3 Slope conveyor system entered the deckhead building, delivering the ore to the secondary crushing plant. To the right of it is the old No. 3 deckhead, used to hoist ore from underground prior to the installation of the conveyor system, and the forwarding conveyor which moved the ore discharged from the secondary crushers to the 7000-ton surge pile. A 42-inch reclaiming conveyor running underneath the surge pile forwarded the ore to the concentrator feed conveyor housed in the building at the right. At the right (to the left of the concentrator building) is a 36-inch float conveyor, which discharged the float product from the washing screens into a bin. From there, it was trucked to waste. (Submarine Miner 5 (1): 7 Jan. 1958)

Timekeeper Jack LeDrew and paymaster Walter McLean distribute pay envelopes at No. 3 Slope pay station in 1956.

The miner receiving his pay here is Gerald Cahill.

The control room for the inter-plant telephone communication system to the underground and trans-island ore conveyor network, 1957. The work here involved looking after the belt system from Flight One in No. 3 Mine, right on up to Flight Ten at the pier. Here, Jim Butt (standing) keeps account of the movement of ore across the island, while Hubert Crane, control room attendant, is on the radio phone to one of the trucks that also transported ore to the pier.

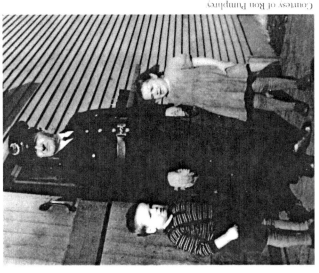

Isaac (Ike) Pumphrey, one of six DOSCO policemen, with two of his children, Gerald and Angela, c. 1949. Because there were only two regular policemen on the Island, the Company policemen (who carried handcuffs but not night sticks or guns) would help them out when circumstances required.

The equipment shown (above) was used by Fred Rose to take the "top seam" ore in the 1950s, long after the mining companies had abandoned surface mining. Such equipment was also used at Dominion Pier to push ore over the cliff for loading into the ore boats. In this 1958 photo, the equipment was on loan from the mining operations to clear the ground for a new ball park on the Green. In the background can be seen Town Square with the Roman Catholic church flanked by the boys' and girls' schools (all of which were later destroyed by fire), buildings on Bennett Street, the water tower, and rows of Company housing.

It takes a special kind of nerve to handle a situation like that and an even greater nerve to remain calm when you yourself are the victim of an accident. Eric recalls a man who was involved in an accident that severed his leg below the knee. The two parts of his leg were attached by only a piece of flesh. While help was being summoned, the man asked for a knife. He then proceeded to finish severing his leg and told one of the men with him to place the cut off leg behind his head for a pillow.

In the early days of the mining operation, many accidents and deaths were caused by "missed holes." These were holes plugged with dynamite that had been missed or had not fired when the blasters went through. Later, a driller might unknowingly penetrate a missed hole and set off an explosion. This is probably what happened one day when a man was literally blown to pieces. It is said that his son, who worked in the same area, had to take up the only part of him that could be found, his fingers. After the funeral, the son went back to work there again.[84] This type of accident was rare in later years but, unfortunately, did happen occasionally right up to the end of operations, as illustrated here by Len Gosse:

> One young feller, I believe he was about thirty year old, thirty-one year old. He blowed up. He and another man, they had the drill sot up, and the other man shook his light and the young feller stopped. And the other man says, "Hold on now till I pulls up and takes that lump out of the way." On back of the lump there was nothing but a full load of powder. And when he started in drilling, it struck there. The lump popped out of the way, and she went right in this hole, into about fifteen plugs of dynamite. And the whole works come right down across the aisle where the young feller was at and the explosion killed him. And the other

man, he never got hurt. The big drill throwed the whole thing right up over his head and pitched on the other side of him. If she had of dropped, come down like that, it would have killed the two of them.

Clayton Basha remembers that same accident and how it affected him:

That incident, I'll never forget it. On that particular day I was doing maintenance, and I was repairing what you call a jumbo drill. A jumbo drill is a huge piece of equipment and it takes two men to operate it, in other words, two men drilling at the one time and it runs by air. You have what you call a jack hammer. What operated that jack hammer was a chain. It was called a feed chain. And I was repairing the feed chain for Bill Vickers and Charlie O'Leary. While I was repairing the drill, we hears this big bang and I mean a bang. I come off the ground, not that the sound was an unusual noise, it was just that it came so sudden. Because down in the mines, if they get a large, huge piece of ore when they blast, sometimes this huge, big hunk of ore don't bust up with the blast and the machinery can't handle it. What they'll do then is go in and just probably put one hole into it with a small plug of dynamite and they'll blast it, but during the working hour. So this was happening all the time. But, of course, if they did this, the foreman would make sure there was nobody around the area, you know, safety precautions, nobody was going to walk into the area. The men would be watching.

Anyway, there was this big blast and the next thing, Bill Jardine, I'll never forget it, he was the foreman on shift, and he come over and he called Bill Vickers and

Charlie O'Leary to one side and he said something to them. Now, I didn't know what it was, but I knew after. And the three of them started walking away. And I don't know why he didn't say nothing to me, [if it was] where I was so young, or he didn't want me, or he had enough help. And I, like a fool, chased them, you know. I walked behind them. But anyway, when I came around the corner, around the rib, they had the victim on the ground, on a stretcher, but they had him covered up. I couldn't see nothing like, you know. And I was right flustered. I can remember myself saying, "What do you want me to do? What do you want me to do?"

And I could see poor buddy, the driller, he was sot down on the side of the rib. He had a hard hat with a peak on it, there was all different styles, and the peak was gone off [his hat], and there was blood running down his face, but he was sitting up. And now, like I say, they usually have that buddy, I suppose, for all their lifetime while they're working. But still in all, I couldn't think immediately of who was under that blanket, you know. Now it didn't take me long to find out. But I knew. It was just the way things were, I was so flustered. And, like I say, I can hear myself saying to Bill Jardine, "What do you want me to do? What do you want me to do?" So now, the stretcher was the cloth one with the two handles, and it took four people to carry it. And he said, "You get ahold of that now and give us a hand to get him out." And we got him out and got him to the surface and that. But then, after that, especially when I'd be on the twelve to eight shift, and when I'd be on the twelve to eight shift, I was mainly working by myself. Now, what I mean by working by myself would be, we'd be just standing by waiting for something to break down. And I was always, if I saw a light coming in a distance, I don't know, I was tense, I was uptight and it was on my mind, I'd say, a good eight or nine months, it could be a year, before it went away completely. He was about thirty-six then and a likeable feller, too, I'll tell you, a really nice person. Everybody liked him. That was a sad day on the Island. Like I say, everybody knew him and liked him.

In the last few years that the mines were in operation, Eric was asked to take the job of trying to find ways of preventing the accidents that had been on the increase. He has thought a lot about what causes accidents:

Most of them, if you trace them, most of them were man-made accidents. I'll give you one case of a feller. His job was, there was a little sally, off-grade sallied down, and when the trip used to go there, she'd stop. His job was to hook a little cable onto it, pull it out of there, and he had nothing else to do only just sit down until that come out. He was a great friend of mine. So this day he gets an idea, there's a piece of ground hanging off, so he gets the bar to pull it down. But he didn't see the cap was on the piece of ground. That came down and killed him. It was just a matter of the man with nothing to do, and he had no business to use the bar. That was one case. Another case is gambling. A man driving a shovel and the face cleaner told him the piece of ground was bungy [loose but still in place]. So he got up on the boom of the shovel and put a wedge in, a piece of wood to wedge it, because when it starts to come it's too late. So he was killed on the shovel.

Foremen were compelled to take first-aid classes so that, in the event of an accident and while awaiting medical assistance, some help could be given on the spot. It was sometimes an hour or longer before the injured could be gotten to the surface. Until 1927, when a man was hurt in the mines, he was conveyed through the streets to the Company's First Aid Station in an open wagon, which had a box about eight inches high, filled with hay. The First Aid Station had only four beds. Each man paid thirty cents a month for medical services. This entitled him to go to the Company doctor and receive treatment, medicines and bandages. In December 1927, the Company acquired a horse-drawn ambulance, which was driven by Arthur Clark. It remained in use until 1948 when Bert Rideout bought a motor ambulance and took over the contract with the Company. The ambulance service was handled by Frank Pendergast from 1965 to 1966. Not all of the accidents attended to were of a life and death nature, as is illustrated by the following narrative:

> One time Arthur went to No. 6. A feller hurted, see, so he got a call. When he got a call, he had to go to what they called the barn down in the slope. He'd go and pick them up. So buddy had his foot hurted, see. And I suppose, the poor old bastard, his feet were dirty. And he belonged to down on the Green. And when they got down to the Green, he opened the doors on the back and got out. And the ambulance went on. Arthur didn't know he was gone. And when he went over to back the horses into the surgery doors, old Dr. Lynch came out and opened the door, and not a soul. And Arthur had to go back on the Green and look for buddy, and found him back home washing his feet.[85]

Mining accidents were sometimes sensed before they happened, either by the miner himself, or by some member of his family. One miner, who had left his house to go to work one morning, is said to have returned and kissed his wife after having gone only a short distance. He was killed that day by a rock fall. When his wife told acquaintances about the good-bye kiss, it was surmised that he had had a premonition of his own death.[86]

Eric's father, Stewart Luffman, was killed in an early morning explosion on August 22, 1916. He and his men were working special twelve-hour shifts while drilling the main slope for No. 3 Mine, and were just finishing up a shift when this accident happened:

> My mother knew. She went to bed and all of a sudden she woke, and she never did before. Something on her mind. This was early in the night. She got up and came down, and she stayed downstairs because she knew there was something wrong. But my father wasn't expected home until half-past seven. And the Salvation Army Captain was there before that. When she see him come to the door, she knew exactly what he was going to tell her.

Eric recalls two occasions when he had uneasy feelings about being in the mines:

> I remember one time in the late '20s, I got so nervous that I wouldn't go to bed until Jack, my stepfather, was home. He was blasting and used to come home ten o'clock. Wouldn't go to bed. I had to make sure he was home. And every day I'd go in the pit, I'd be frightened to death. And this day Sam Cobb was killed, and then it left me just like that.

This same feeling came over him again prior to the deaths of Randall Skanes and James Butler, who were killed by runaway ore cars in October 1949:

> I was working in No. 6 then, and I went to go home in the evening and Randall said to me, "Stay down. We're going to do something with the road." I said, "I can't do it. I got to go home. I got something to do." I got home and Stella says, "What's wrong with you?" I said, "I don't know. I'm after losing my appetite." That was about six o'clock in the evening. "There's something wrong, Stella," I says, "but I don't know what it is." So I called up to see if Jack was home. He was home. All the family was home. By and by, Jeanie come home from Charlie Cohen's store. She worked to Charlie Cohen's then. She said, "Mr. Skanes and Mr. Butler was killed in No. 6 this evening."

Len had a similar thing happen to him on June 5, 1964, when he stayed home from work because of intuition, perhaps saving his own life. On that day, a man in his section was killed by a cave-in:

> This man, he got killed in the section where I worked. And that day I stayed off, never went to work. And he was killed that morning, eleven o'clock. I woke up six o'clock as usual. I said, "Nina, you got the lunch rigged for me yet?" She says, "No." I says, "Okay, I'm not going to work, not today. I can't go to work. There's something wrong somewhere. I can't go to work today." And he only had two more shifts to work and he'd be finished in the mines. He and his wife were going away to Galt. He had his notice and everything put in with the Company, put in a week's notice, and he got killed Thursday.

On another occasion, Eric's ability to sense danger saved the lives of two men. One night he and Bob Basserman, an efficiency expert brought in near the end of operations to cut down on the work force, went to investigate a problem. Two men, who did not speak English very well, had shut off their drills. They were trying to communicate what was wrong when Eric sensed that something was about to happen. He told the men to come with him but, because of their lack of understanding of the language, they did not move. So Eric told Basserman what he wanted him to do:

> So I took one feller, and I said, "Bob, take the other feller by the arm and let's lead them out of here." "What for?" he said. "When we gets out now I'll tell you," I said. "Don't talk. Don't make no noise at all. Just take them by the hand and just smile and keep going out of here."

They were no sooner out when the spot where they had just been caved in. Basserman asked him how he had known what was going to happen. "'I smelled it, Bob,' I said. I don't know how I knew. Instinct, maybe, or intuition."

While he never sensed an accident about to happen, Harold remembers a strange dream he once had after a man was killed in the mines. The scene of the accident had been closed down for a long time, and now they were going to go in there again to work it. Harold was one of the crew. He was not aware of how the man had died but, one night shortly after he started working there, he had a dream in which he saw everything in full detail. His boss knew all about the accident and, when Harold related his dream to him, he confirmed that it was exactly how it had happened.

There are many similarities between the traditions and practices of Wabana miners and miners in other parts of the world. For example, it was a common practice in mines all over North America, as well as England and other European countries, for all the men to walk off the job when a man was killed. There seems to have been no one rule in the Bell Island mines. One miner said that this may have happened occasionally, but not usually. When a man was hurt, those who worked with him would stop working to bring him up out of the mines. When a man died in the mines, it would be only his fellow workers and friends who would attend the funeral.

However, several other miners said that if a man was killed, the other men in that mine usually stopped work. Some said the men would stay off until after the funeral, while others said that they would stay off for one day.[87] George, Len and Clayton have the following recollections:

> I remember one day, I was working on the Scotia Line, over in No. 6 Bottom, about one or half past one o'clock I think it was. And 'twas an accident in the mines. And when anything happened in the mines, it would go like that (snaps his fingers), spread like wildfire. And this evening about one or one-thirty, the news come up out of the mines that there were two men squat to death by a fall of ground. Called the whole shebang off. All the mines closed where the two men were killed, you know.[88]

> The men would close it down theirselves. They wouldn't work. If they knowed that anyone got killed, say for instance, Leander Gosse got killed seven o'clock at night and nobody never knowed it. They never told nobody, only them fellers was in that headway. If they had ringed and said they knocked off working, we would have stopped and that's it. But they never sent in to us. If they hadda sent in to us, we would have stopped too. But the next day, everything was off.

> We all stopped work when someone was killed. That was just for that day, then you'd continue on. It didn't

matter what time that happened, there'd be no night shift, there'd be no 12:00 shift. It would be the next shift that you'd start again. Once it happened, there would be no sense, no one would be able to do anything. The whole mine would come up. Lots of times you would be home and you'd see all the men coming off work, probably dinner time and you'd say, "There must be an accident." For some reason or other, no matter what part of the Island, everybody knew. I can't say just as it happened, but it wouldn't be very long, within the hour. Everybody would be in a lull for, I don't know, a week, week and a half. Then she'd go on just the same as if nothing ever happened.

A man who was hit by a fall of ground while working with Albert did not die immediately, so the other men continued to work when he was taken out. When it was learned that he died on the way to the surface, the others all quit working.

It was the custom in the Wabana mines to mark a cross on a rib near the spot where a man was killed. This served as a memorial to the deceased. It probably also had the subliminal effect of making the miners more aware of their own mortality and, thus, more careful in their jobs.

It was commonly believed on Bell Island that it was extremely unlucky for a woman to go down into the mines.[89] Many people believed that if a woman went down, someone would be killed shortly thereafter, as exemplified by the following narrative:

Years ago, it was strictly taboo for a woman to go underground. They had this belief that if a woman went underground, there was sure to be an accident. This sort of thing was built up in their minds. The older mine captains, they didn't want anyone whatsoever to bring a woman in the underground workings cause there was sure to be an accident, and sometimes someone was killed. It usually happened that if a woman came down, probably a week or a month after that, someone got killed. They'd say, "That's what happened. He brought that one down. He shouldn't have had her around here at all."

You know, it wasn't until about fifteen years before the mines closed down that women were really allowed, given permission, to go down underground. I worked underground for about eighteen years. Even when I worked down there, if you see a woman coming, my God, it was terrible. Most of the women you would get going underground was probably women who worked on a magazine, or some paper somewhere, you know. She came down to see what the mines was like and probably get a story on that. But it was strictly taboo. It didn't matter a darn where she was working on a [news]paper or what she was working on. It was still the same thing. They didn't like to see her there.[90]

The miners would not go so far as to walk off the job over the intrusion of a woman into their territory but, according to George:

That was considered bad luck, for a woman to go down in the mines. The men didn't want that at all. They more or less kicked up a fuss if they knew that there was a woman going to go down in the mines.

Len recalled actual accidents that the miners believed were direct results of women visiting the mines:

A man never wanted to see a woman come in the mines. Every time a woman went down in the mines, there was a man killed. That's the truth, too. It really happened. When they were putting the belts in, there was a Canadian, a French-Canadian. Two women went down in the mines to see what was going on, with the captain of the mines there, Mr. Tommy Gray. He brought two women down. They were looking at the new pockets and the new tiplet and what was going on, cause me brother, he was there looking after it all. And someone said, "Here they goes again. We'll have it in a couple of days' time."

Len went on to say that it was two nights later that the body of the man, who had been run over and dismembered by the man tram as described earlier, was found. However, the curse did not end there:

There was a young feller, he used to work with us. He was an orphan and the Welfare reared him up. He come down in the mines when the belts was going in. And he was an auto mechanic, see. And he was doing something and shoved his head in under the belt like that and someone shoved on the switch. Cut the head off him. That's where the two women just went down before that. That was two men dead. And before Leander Gosse died, there was a woman went down in the mines. And there was one down before Paddy Kelly. There was one down there before Walter Rees. And there was a woman went down in the mines when Martin Sheppard got killed. And there was a woman went down in the mines when Hayward George, he got killed. Every time a woman went in the mines, a man got killed.

It seems that womankind was not the only supposed jinx for the miners. A certain mine official occasionally visited Bell Island to inspect the operation. It was said of him, "every time he came to Bell Island, this is an actual fact, somebody was killed. That's an honest fact." None of the reports about this man's amazing attribute mention how he, himself, died. He was a passenger on the steamer *Caribou* when it was torpedoed on October 14, 1942 while travelling from Nova Scotia to Newfoundland. He was one of the 137 victims of that tragedy.[91]

Some miners believed that to call a person who had overslept would be tantamount to calling him to his death.[92] One miner remembers what a buddy of his told him about a time when he called another miner and regretted it afterwards:

> "I called this feller. He was slept in that morning and I called him. By hell," he said, "that day he was killed. So," he said, "I'd never call a feller again." And somebody said that happened to another man too, when he was killed, he was called that morning.[93]

A belief in other parts of the world is that it is bad luck for a miner to return home for something he has forgotten. Len tells an amusing anecdote about a Wabana miner that could be rooted in this superstition:

> A cousin of mine, he lived over on the Green, see. He worked in No. 4, and he had a good mile to walk, see. So this morning he gets out of bed kind of late, and he gets up and scravels on his clothes, puts on his boots and instead of taking his lunch, he grabbed the clock and put it under his arm. He took off, this is a true story, and he took off and he got up as far as Suicide Dam, and he heard the clock ticking. He looked down like this. "To hell with this," he said. He took the clock and fired it out in the dam and went back home. He stayed home that day.

Another indicator of bad luck around the world is the common crow. A neighbour was on his way to work one morning just as

Eric was leaving his house. Suddenly the man turned around and started back home. "What's wrong?" Eric asked him. "Bloody crow flew over my head," he said. "I can't go in the pit today."

Whether or not the men dwelt on the danger that was an intrinsic part of their lives, there is no doubt that they sensed it to some degree as they went about their work. It is not surprising then, to find that some of them would use a familiar and easily accessible object, thought by many people everywhere to have the power to fend off misfortune and bring good luck, as their talisman. Belief in horseshoes as such a good luck charm was common among the miners, and you even had to know the proper way to hang one: "You had to hang them with the open end up or the luck would fall out." They were hung mostly on posts in the dry houses where the men ate. If a miner found one on the footwall, he would nail it up on a nearby post. One man reports that he did that himself "with no belief into it that it was going to bring me luck."

Fortunately, not all the mishaps that occurred in the mines ended in tragedy. Some comical stories, such as this one related by Eric, came out of accidents that ended happily:

> The mines had a pitch of 13 percent in some places, and there would be always water left on the low side, you see, from the drills and so forth. And we had a feller, this day, putting on a piece of rope around the shovel head, and he slipped off and got down and got his feet wet. "Well, well, well," he said, "now, look what I got to do now. Right in the middle of winter I got to wash my feet."

While it is understandable that when a man was killed his fellow workers would be shocked and aggrieved, Eric tells of a man who seems to have been less concerned about losing his buddy than he was with the thought of a pair of good boots going to waste:

> Fred Newton was working with a feller one time, and Fred got a crack on the head. Knocked him out, stunned him for a minute. When he come to, his buddy had his boots off. "What are you doing with me boots?" Fred asked him, and this feller says, "I thought you were dead, buddy."

Where there are unnatural deaths, there are often reports of ghost sightings. Several miners say that buddies of theirs told of seeing ghosts of miners who had been killed in the mines: "They thought they saw the ghost alongside them drilling." George tells of an experience his brother, Leander, had in the early 1950s involving the ghost of a dead miner, a driver who had been killed in the headway in No. 3 Mine. Some time after the driver's death, Leander got a job working the graveyard shift there. After midnight he would be there by himself until morning. After all the men had gone up, it was a lonely place, but he did not seem to mind. Then one morning, at half-past two, George's telephone rang:

> This was Leander, my brother. I said, "Where are you to, Leander?" He said, "B'y, I'm down in the mines, No. 3 Mines." He said, "I'm down here by meself now. I don't know whether it was my imagination, or whether it was true or what, but I was going up the headway and I saw the man [the dead driver] in the chair, and I got that lonely I had to give you a call, b'y."

Leander found out afterwards that his predecessor in that job had had the same experience:

> One night he was coming from somewhere, from getting a mug-up, and going up the headway, he seen

the driver sitting in the chair. He said that before long, just like that, there was nothing there. He applied for another job and got away from there.

When Leander got the job, the man he replaced did not tell him of his experience. He only found out after he saw the ghost himself. He left the job then as well.

Ghosts of miners were not restricted to the underground slopes where they had worked. A woman, whose home was close to the collar of No. 2 Mine, recalled an occasion when she, her husband and son were playing a game of cards with three other women. No. 2 had been closed down for some time so, when one of the women noticed someone near the slope, everyone became curious and went to the window to look:

> They couldn't believe what they saw, for men were coming up out of the slope, two by two, and going past the check house. They counted from ninety to a hundred men. After the last one had come up, the men went to check. The slope was still barred, and no trace of these men could be seen, not even their footprints in the snow.[94]

If the circumstances are right, even when a ghost is not actually seen, an individual may come to expect a sighting, as in the following case:

> A man who had worked on the haulage, or steam hoist, for many years, hauling out the loaded ore cars to be dumped, passed away. One night sometime later, the watchman on duty heard the machinery start, even though he knew no one was supposed to be working there at that hour. It soon stopped, so he believed it was his imagination but, shortly after, he heard it start again and stop as before. He felt now that it was not his

imagination, so he decided to investigate. As fast as he could, he ran up the flight of steps to the building, fully expecting to see his late friend with his hand working the lever, but there was no one there and everything was quiet. It was puzzling, but belief in ghosts was not unusual, so the watchman was, to say the least, skeptical. He waited for his relief to come on duty and together they examined the haulage to see if there really was a ghost or if something else had caused the machinery to start up. They discovered that a leaky valve was allowing steam to escape so that enough pressure was building up to start the machine, but not to keep it going. Men who were of a more nervous disposition might have fled the scene to disseminate the story of "the ghost of the haulage."[95]

In a similar case, a man believed that he had been dogged by a ghost, but was embarrassed a few days later to find that his "ghost" had been something else:

> One time, in No. 6, the horses used to be brought up only at Christmas. The rest of the year they weren't brought up, but on weekends the stable boss used to have to go down and feed the horses. So he was coming up this weekend after the feeding and didn't see a light, but he did hear foot steps behind him. Now he got nervous and used to stop. And when he'd stop, the foot steps would stop. And he went on again and eventually came to the building. And when he looked back he couldn't see anything. He was convinced a ghost had followed him up. But on Monday morning, he learned that one of the horses had gotten out of the stable and chased him up, and they had to look for it. So that must have been his ghost.[96]

It is easy to understand belief in ghosts underground, considering the surroundings and general atmosphere in which the miners worked. Following is an illustration of how easy it was to get lost in the mines and some of the things a man alone had to worry about.

George got lost in the mines shortly after he started working underground, around 1930. One day he was told he would have to go "in west" to work. This was about two miles in from where he had been working all along. He had no trouble getting in there because he simply went with a couple of other men who knew the way. As it happened, he had an "early shift" that day. In other words, he finished loading early, so he was able to go on home before the normal quitting time. He went to the dry house, or lunch room, to wait for some of the men to finish so that he could go out with them, but grew tired of waiting and decided to try and find his own way out:

> I took the carbide lamp out of my cap, put it on my finger and went on, happy as a lark because I had an early shift. I started off and I kept going, going, going. Finally I didn't hear a sound of anything. Didn't hear the sound of cars or nothing at all. And I stopped. The rats were everywhere, darting around. I started to look around the place, and I said, "My God, where am I?" I said, "I'm astray. Now," I said, "which direction can I go to get back on the right track again?" I said, "I'll try this way." And I went on. I didn't know where I was going, and I went into an old room that was worked out and brought up against a solid face of iron ore. I couldn't get out. I turned around and went in another direction. All I was afraid was my lamp would go out, 'cause I didn't have too much carbide. I'd be in the dark, because there were no electric lights, no nothing.

I went in another direction and went into another old

room, went on in, in, in, in, in, and I brought up against a solid face of iron ore again and couldn't get out. "Gentle God," I said, "where am I to?" I came out. I said, "In God's name, I'll go in this direction." I kept on going, going, going. I said, "I'm finished. They'll never find me." Now in the dark when you see a light in the distance, it will be very, very small. I kept on going, and going, and by and by I thought I saw a little light. "My God," I said, "I wonder is that a light? What is it?" And I kept on going for it. And the farther I went ahead, this little light started to get bigger. I said, "Thanks be to God. I think that's a light." And I kept on going for it. And I went right back from where I started. That's what I did.

This story and the next show that some parts of the mines were spooky and creepy. The main areas were well lit but, in a lot of places, the only light was the one you had with you. If you had anything on your mind, travelling alone through these unlit areas did not help matters, as Clayton found out.

When he was still living at home, Clayton's grandmother lived with the family. She had been with them ever since he was a small child. As young children, he and his siblings used to play tricks on her, such as making the alarm clock ring so that she would think it was the telephone and get out of bed to answer it. Then they would crawl under her bedclothes, lie still until she got back into bed and then tap her on the back to make her scream with fright. His grandmother had been bedridden for quite a while by the time he was working in the mines. One Saturday night, he was sitting at home with his mother when they heard a thump upstairs. They found his grandmother on the floor in the bathroom with her hand clasped around the chrome supporting leg of the wash basin. She was still alive, but they could not get her hand from around this leg. His mother called this the "death hold." Clayton had to unscrew the leg and slip it out of her hand that way. At the time, he was working on the continuous operations, and he had to go to work the next morning, even though it was a Sunday. And, of course, he was worried about his grandmother. He was no sooner down in the mines when he got the call saying she had died and he had to go back up again:

> Where I was working at that time, you could go from No. 3 up to No. 4. This is where we were working at. Now to get from No. 3 to No. 4, you had to go through a place called "Dog's Hole Hill." This was a place where you had to duck down, you wouldn't have to crawl. This was in the mines, to get from one mine to the other. No. 4 then had no deckhead. The ore from No. 4 used to come down to No. 3 and go on up that way. So, to get back to the surface, I had to come back to No. 3 and come down over this Dog's Hole Hill. And coming down the Dog's Hole Hill, all this was coming in my mind. It was only foolish; it was only stuff running through your mind. I figured she was going to come and get me for all this old foolish stuff that we'd be doing [when we were children]. I couldn't wait until I saw the first light. The next lighted area you'd see was the warehouse. And when I saw the first light, I was right relieved.

These stories show that when a man was alone underground, he was really alone. Eric puts it this way:

> Everything was silence. You never know what silence is until you get underground and it's quiet, dead silence, grave silence, fearful.

There were even some miners who got to the point where they had to quit mining because working in that silence bothered them so much. Eric tells the reason his stepfather decided that mining was not the work for him:

> He was down in the nighttime, quiet, deadly quiet, loading away. No one there, perhaps by himself, and he heard the sand, the sea, rolling above him. No. 6 only had two hundred feet above, between the roof of the mine and the ocean floor. And he was loading away, and he heard the beach rocks rolling.

With this kind of loneliness and stories being told of ghosts of dead miners, it can be expected that there would be some practical jokers who would take advantage of this situation to set the scene for their pranks. One such prank caused another nervous man to give up mining:

> This story is true and concerns a miner who was easily agitated. On this particular occasion, a fellow workman stripped himself of his clothes and hid in an area where a workman had previously been killed, knowing that his intended victim would pass nearby on his return from the mines. When he heard the victim approaching, he began to moan and make peculiar noises, giving the victim the impression that he was seeing the ghost of the departed one in anguish. The unfortunate man got such a fright that he became mentally disturbed and gave up his job, never to work underground another day.[97]

Ghosts were not the only supernatural beings observed by Wabana mine workers. Many of these men believed in the existence of fairies. A man who worked at No. 4 compressor claimed that one night, when he was on duty, the fairies visited him. He described them as little men about three feet tall, all wearing red stocking caps on their heads. When he began cursing, they went away. And, at a certain time each year in an area near the mines, people were said to have observed a fairy celebration with dancing and merry making.[98]

One miner gives the following vivid account of something that happened while he was working on the surface around 1918:

> Meself and me buddy were working on the buckets one day, you know. We had to wait for the ore to come up and dump it. It's getting on in the morning, and he says to me at about eleven o'clock, "Will you cover for me for ten minutes. I gotta go down in the woods for a while." I said, "Okay, Jim." So he goes on down in the woods. Time goes by. Half an hour, hour. Still no Jim. I says to meself, "That son of a bitch is down there sleeping." So I rounded up a couple of me buddies and we went down for him, but we couldn't find him. So we came back and told the foreman on the job, and he goes and tells the big boss. I can't remember his name now. Anyway, this is something big now, you know, 'cause Jim was never one to run away from work. The boss comes and forms a search party of about fifty men and we still couldn't find him. Then he sent someone to get the police. It wasn't the RCMP then. It was the local fellers. My son, we searched high and low. Had people come from town and everything but, you know, we couldn't find Jim.
>
> This kept up for two or three days. Then one day when I was back to work, up walked Jim outta the woods, beaming like an electric bulb. I says, "Where have you been?" He says, "Where have I been? I been down in the woods. That's where I been. Sorry to be so long but, Jesus, no need to be mad. I was only gone an hour. I just met the nicest little people. You go on to lunch now and I'll take over." "Take over," says I. "You

son of a, where have you been this past three days? We was all worried to death over you." "What are you talking about?" says Jim. "'Tis only twelve o'clock. Listen. There goes the whistle." And so it was twelve o'clock, but three days later.

Jim was telling me later that he met a whole pile of little people, and they had food and beer and danced and played the accordion. Real friendly, he said. Well, it was some going on when everyone found out he was back, 'cause we all thought he was dead, you see. After falling off the back of the Island or something. Yes sir, he was the only one that was ever treated that good by the fairies. But people always thought him a little queer after that. And you know, he swore that was the truth right up until he died. And you know something else, I believe him.[99]

EIGHT

LIFE AFTER DOSCO

When I left the mines over on the Island,
I wouldn't go nowhere else in the mine.

Albert Higgins

THE MEN WHOSE stories are featured in this book all felt that the mining life on Bell Island had been a good one for the most part. They all said that if they were younger and had the opportunity to do it all again, they would. The physical working conditions were better than in a lot of other mines. This was confirmed for Eric Luffman in 1954 when the Company sent him on a tour of mining operations in the United States to see what kinds of equipment were being used elsewhere:

> I went down in five or six mines belonging to Tennessee Coal and Iron. They were just outside of Birmingham, Alabama. I went down in four or five mines in Missouri. And there wasn't one mine that I went into that was fit for a human being to work in. It took me three days to get the dust out of my eyes after I got out of Ozark Ore.

In one mine there was so much water, the men had to wear chest-high rubber waders. In another mine, if the power failed, the men had to run for their lives because of the carbon monoxide that would quickly accumulate in the mine. The superintendent of that mine later came to Bell Island to purchase some equipment that was for sale there. When Eric showed him around No. 3, his guest remarked, "This is a different place altogether. How in the hell do you do it?" Eric elaborates:

> You could go down in No. 3 with your slippers on. You wouldn't get your feet wet. I've seen men who never lost a shift for years, they liked to work that well down in No. 3 Mines. It was a picnic as far as we were concerned. We had one superintendent and his policy was: treat the man like he was your own son and you can't go wrong. You cannot go wrong. Well, that's what made No. 3 so good. The old man, Gray, was very, very, very cautious. Very cautious. He worked a lot of time in the coal mines, and he learned an awful lot of tricks. And then, he was the kind of feller who had a tremendous respect for his fellow man.

Things began to go bad on Bell Island in the late 1950s. Markets began to go elsewhere, such as Labrador, when it was found that ore there could be produced less expensively and with fewer impurities. Steel mills were converting to new equipment and methods for which Wabana ore was less suitable. The parent company, DOSCO, under which Wabana had prospered, was taken over, first by A. V. Roe Canada Limited and soon after that by Hawker Sidley Canada Limited. New people were brought in from England and mainland Canada in an attempt to find ways of cutting costs to make the operation more competitive:

> All of a sudden, the bottom dropped out of the bag;

new management didn't know what they were talking about. Mining is just as safe as walking the road, but you must follow the rules, not the rules of government, but the laws of nature. Mother Nature will allow you to take just what you want if you don't stretch it too far. If you do, something will break.

There were many complaints about these late years of the Wabana mining operation, and the new people who suddenly appeared on the scene. Outsiders had always been imported for professional jobs in the mines. Even though there was always a certain amount of enmity for these people, those who came during the final years seemed to attain greater heights of resentment than ever before. The reason for this becomes clear when one understands why these men were brought in. Whereas earlier experts were hired for traditional jobs such as mining engineers and mining supervisors, these new people were hired to improve the mining operation. Their jobs involved trimming unnecessary spending, finding ways to cut inefficient practices and recommending other cost-saving procedures. In the process, it seems, the human factor was overlooked. Eric continues:

> The last couple of years we worked, we had a lot of accidents, first time in our lives. I was section foreman for a great many years, a lot of years, I don't know how many, perhaps fifteen years. I never had a fatal accident on my section. I had one feller lost his leg, and that was just pure stupidness. The last year No. 3 worked, 1965, we had three fatal accidents, and we had thirteen more men broke up. And the whole lot was due to too much ore being taken from the support pillars. They sent a maniac in and he started taking a piece out of here, and a piece out of here, and a piece out of here, and here, all the way back. It was easy to get.

But, you see, finally it began to take pressure. We had sixteen hundred feet above us, not counting the weight of the ocean, and that pillar was the only thing you had to protect you. So we had a feller one time, let's say this is a pillar here and he was mining here, taking off too much. A piece, this was square, what we call a corner, and we had a feller on a Joy Loader taking this out of here now, and this corner began to bust. And finally this popped off out here, and a young feller got killed underneath the Joy Loader. It popped off with weight. You couldn't judge it at all because the weight was so great. There were areas that were all mined out by the room and pillar method, but this boss went back over it and she began to get weak.

These new people were there for the short term and did not have a vested interest in the Island or its people. Indeed, any sentimental attachment to the miners was undesirable, as the results of their work often meant the closing down of unprofitable sections of the mines and a subsequent loss of jobs. Eric believes their presence led to the antagonism and alienation of the miners:

I have no ill will against anybody. But I've met so many people think they know so much, they must think either I am bloody stupid or they don't know what's wrong with me, why I can't think like them. In the dying years of Bell Island they came in, now we had lots of men come from the mainland, come from the coal mines, excellent miners and good men to work with, but they brought them in on the last from hell's creeks, from all over. They came in with chips on their shoulders, you could see them, with the very worst possible thoughts in their minds of Newfoundlanders. You could tell them nothing and, on the last of it, nobody would tell them nothing. The men, on the last, just done what they were told and nothing more than what they were told. You can't run that kind of a job.

They came here from hard-rock mines, where you've got to chase gold and silver all over the place like a snake. This stuff, iron ore, is almost like a mat laid down and covered over. But hard-rock mines, you may have a piece of gold here today and you mightn't see another piece for five months, but you chase the little veins and put in your test rods. We didn't need none of that, but on the last of it we had everything. They just thought they were into a gold mine, some of those fellers, but it's not gold. The mining is completely different from hard-rock mining. I had a feller who come to work with me one time told me he never used a facebar in his life. He worked in hard-rock all his lifetime. They wanted to condemn the facebar as soon as they got here. And in some cases they cut out the four-foot bar that was used along the stand. But they were hard-rock miners. They probably were all right around gold and silver, chasing stuff all over the place and, of course, they could not admit to the likes of me that they were wrong. That would be an insult to the Canadian dignity, to admit that a Newfoundlander knew more than they did. No way in the world could you ever get them to admit that.

I remember one time I had a feller working with me, as a matter of fact, I worked under him for years, a good feller, Fred Newton. Fred used to send down a few pieces of timber in the nighttime along with the supplies and spread it along where we were going to use it the next night, see, because if he didn't, the timber-men would have to go down and wait for the shift to go down in the mornings and then come back and go to the deck and get their timber, and half the night was gone. There was no danger in the world because it was thrown down by the side of the track, and it was no danger at all. So, this day, this boss was walking down, and he come up and said, "I wants that timber shifted." So poor old Fred tried to explain to him. But he said, "That's all I've heard since I come here is 'can't.' Shift it." Newton took it to heart and went home and never come back for a month. The first son of a bitch that ever bawled at Fred Newton in his life. Nobody ever needed to bawl at Fred Newton. Fred Newton was forty times a better man than the man that was talking to him. So anyway, this same boss came along to me after, and he said, "I'm going to send my son down on C shift with the timber crew." I said, "All right." So he come back up to me the next day, and he said, "Do you know that your timber crew don't get to work until three or four o'clock in the morning waiting for timber?" "You're the man who caused that," I said. "Do you remember you yelled at Fred Newton?"

This is the type of man we had to deal with on the last of it, you see. And the men hated him, hated him. And that was unusual for the men. I'll tell you the truth. I went to work on a drill, and the mine captain gave me an eighteen-inch Stillson wrench. During the fourteen years I worked on the drill, I guess he replaced the jaw and the nut and the frame perhaps twice or three times. But I had that wrench when I finished with the drill and passed it over to the next man. When we closed down, you couldn't keep anything in the mines, absolutely nothing. It was stolen as fast as we took it down. The whole thing changed overnight. Thievery that we never knew anything of. A timber-man could stick an axe in a piece of wood and come back two weeks later, it would still be there. And on the last, it cost us forty thousand dollars a year for tools alone. The men didn't like their jobs, didn't like the people they were working for. That's what caused all the accidents. Foremen not allowed to be doing what they should be doing. Working on a note and what was on that note, that's what they done and nothing else. And that note was made out for every foreman every day up in the office, pass it over to them. No use in telling the men to do anything else or this feller would fire you just like that.

Clayton tells what the last few shifts were like for him and his buddies:

The last three or four shifts we worked, we knew that the end was here. On the timecards, we'd draw pictures of fellers sitting on the toilet and a feller lying in the bed. Because they weren't going to fire us anyway. We were gone, you know.

Now first when I went to work with the maintenance department, we were issued tools. But there was never any notice put up saying to turn them in. So everyone was going around [saying], "What about the tools? What about the tools?" Now in the meantime, it was only the basic toolbox. There was no big amount of money, but it was all right to have around home. Anyway, so I started bringing mine home bit by bit, this was the last two or three days, in my lunch box. And everybody started doing the same thing. Anyway, I had this beautiful, elaborate toolbox. I can see it now, a big, red feller, and he'd open up and there'd be all your drawers. And this was all that was left. I couldn't take chances, I didn't want to take chances of walking out to the gate with this big, red toolbox. And my buddy said to me, he said, "If you don't take that, I'll take it." And sure enough, he did. He walked right out to the gate. Now when you stop to think about it, the security, he's not going to stop you, you know. You're going home now. This is your last day. You're finished. What did he care? He didn't care what you took. So, anyway, Gerald went on with the toolbox and I said, "You bugger."

The Company brought in all those experts at the end in an attempt to avert the inevitable. The workers, not able to foresee what was coming, became more angry and frustrated as time went on. Mutilating timecards and stealing tools and other equipment was a way for them to vent their feelings of anger towards the Company for the close-down which, in reality, was brought on by economic circumstances beyond anyone's control.

After the Company pulled out, Premier Smallwood proclaimed that he had a contract on his desk that would see a German firm take over the mining operation on Bell Island. He set up a special radio news broadcast during the 1966 provincial election campaign in which he announced this contract and said that it merely needed his signature to bring the deal to fruition. After winning the election, he revealed that the deal had fallen through. As Eric observed:

> Smallwood made a mistake by saying that the Germans were going to come. People let a whole twelve months go by [with their hopes built up by] that "contract on the desk." People waited for a year, and they spent more money than they should have because they were sure that was going to materialize.

In a 1974 documentary, Mr. Smallwood explained why the deal fell through:

> I tried hard. I worked very hard with the help of the Canadian government and their top-ranking officials, who went with me to Europe. And we negotiated with a big company, one of the last companies in the world using high phosphorus ore. That company, that steel mill, is just on the border of Germany and France. And they were getting a lot of their ore, their main supply of ore, from France. And they were selling a large part of their steel in France. So they'd bring iron ore into Germany and use it in their mill. Bring it in from France and then ship a lot of the steel to France. When the French learned, the French government learned, that this company was negotiating to come to Bell Island and take over Bell Island, they put their foot down very firmly and said, "If you don't take our iron ore, but get it elsewhere, you'll sell no steel in France." So they got scared and called off the whole deal.[100]

Many die-hards remained on the Island for the year or so that it took for the Germans to make up their minds, convinced that their way of life would not have to change after all. They had no reason to believe otherwise. From 1895 until the first major lay-off in 1959, Bell Island had been a growth area and a centre of industry in Conception Bay. Many people had come there to work and moved their families in, while others commuted to the Island on a weekly basis. The mines had gone through some rough times before and had always come back to better times.

At one time there were even two versions of a rhyme about the economic climate of Bell Island which show how its prosperity was viewed one way by the people of the home communities of the commuters and another way by the residents of the Island. The first version shows a reserved acceptance of having to go to Bell Island to find work:

Harbour Grace is a hungry place
And Carbonear is not much better,
So you've got to go to old Bell Isle
To get your bread and butter.

The second version was a proud proclamation by the residents of a boom town who knew when they were well off:

Harbour Grace is a hungry place
And so is Carbonear,
But when you come to old Bell Isle
You're sure to get your share.[101]

In 1961, the Island's population, 95 percent of which depended directly on the mining operation, peaked at 12,281. With lay-offs becoming a common occurrence and rumours of the operation closing down for good in a few years time, people began to leave for Ontario, where jobs were said to be plentiful both in mining and in the factories. One of the places that many Bell Islanders had gravitated towards in the 1950s was Galt, now called Cambridge. During the early 60s, many more went there to work in the factories and to be close to relatives and friends, swelling the population to such an extent that the town was nicknamed "Little Bell Isle." Great numbers of these former Bell Islanders return "home" regularly during vacation time, with hopes of reliving old memories of their earlier lives on "the Rock." Connections between Bell Island and its former residents who now live in Galt/Cambridge are so close that it is said that, when something happens on the Island, half the population of Galt knows about it before it is common knowledge locally.

In spite of the fact that the only industry closed down in 1966 and large numbers of people moved away to find other work, Bell Island did not become a ghost town. This is probably due to its proximity to the province's capital city. A ferry run of fifteen minutes, followed by a short car ride of twenty minutes, brings Bell Islanders to day jobs in St. John's. Thus, a town that was once a place that workers commuted to is now a dormitory town for people who commute to jobs elsewhere. In St. John's, many older miners who felt that they could not pull up stakes and resettle on the Canadian mainland, as many of their friends were doing, found work at government-run institutions as watchmen and security guards. Some of the younger miners found work in trades that were related to the kinds of jobs they had held in the mines, such as driving heavy equipment, mechanical, electrical and construction work, for example. Office staff had little difficulty moving to similar office jobs off the Island.

Another factor that allowed the town to survive was the relative ease with which it was now possible for those who were out of work to obtain social assistance. Whereas, in former times, it would have been deemed socially unacceptable to be "on welfare," after the mines closed down, living "off the government" became a way of life for a large percentage of the population. These people were, in a real sense, cheated out of their livelihoods by factors that were beyond their control. In their and their parents' pre-mining days, they had been, for the most part, fishermen who were masters of their own fate to a certain degree. To supplement their incomes, many found seasonal employment in the lumberwoods in the winter or as sealers in the spring. Some did construction work on the side and most families kept farm animals and vegetable gardens. Mining on Bell Island had been so steady for so long that they had gotten away from this manner of subsistence. They had become spoiled to the extent that, when the mining was taken away from them, they were unable to adjust psychologically to doing anything else. They had put down roots, had made homes and raised families, and now many felt that they were too old to change their way of life.

While the population continues to decline, it was still a relatively healthy 3,075 at the taking of the 2001 Census. Essential services such as schools, churches, service clubs, shops, a town council, and a hospital, which actually served very few mining accidents because it was not built until the mines started to fail, are all "going strong" today. In the first years after the mines closed, the people who stayed behind had little money and less confidence to keep their properties in repair, for they knew that if things did not work out for them, they would have scant hope of recouping any money spent on upkeep. The sad state of property in general, and the barred up houses and shops, all combined to give the town a dilapidated appearance. Today things are looking much better. The people who stayed on the Island are realizing that the world did not come to an end when the Company moved out. Those people who have steady work have come to trust their futures as residents of Bell Island and are spending their earnings on home improvements. Government housing programs are providing new, good quality homes to those who do not have the means to provide their own and are giving assistance to those who live in their original homes, to help them upgrade. Thus, while many isolated mining towns go bust and disappear from the map, Wabana lives on as a suburb of St. John's. And who knows, perhaps one day the world's supply of easily accessible, high-grade iron ore will run out. When it does, Wabana will still be there with its millions of tons of ore, ready to bring boom times once again to Conception Bay.

APPENDIX

The Murals Project

THE MURALS PROJECT was started in 1990 when Brian Burke was operating a mini-golf course on Bell Island and was looking for ways to attract customers to his business. He had seen the CBC television program *On the Road Again* in which the community of Chemainus, British Columbia, was featured. This former logging town just north of Victoria had lost its only industry and was drawing great numbers of tourists to see the large murals depicting the town's history. "I thought of doing a mural on a building next to the golf course. I figured a few people would come by to take a look and at least some of them would stay and play golf," Burke recalls. He started gathering old photographs of the community and mining industry to get an image for his mural but, as he talked to residents and the Town Council about the plan, the idea grew into a project to paint murals on buildings throughout the town, just as had been done in Chemainus. He asked Charlie Bown, who was the deputy Mayor, and Steve Fitzgerald, Robbie Murphy, Betty O'Neill and Bill Whalen to serve on the first Bell Island Murals Project Committee. They approached government agencies to raise the funds to get started. The Town Council, the provincial Department of Development, Enterprise Newfoundland and Labrador, Employment and Immigration Canada, and the Atlantic Canada Opportunities Agency, as well as private individuals, all contributed funds to pay for materials and provide training allowances for the artists.

By the summer of 1991, the project was underway with eight artists, all with local connections, working on the first four murals. The lead artist was John Littlejohn, described in a 1990 *Express* article as a "rising wildlife artist, who has concentrated on painting animals in meticulously technical detail for the last six years." Littlejohn's work had caught the eye of naturalist painter Robert Bateman, and his work entitled "Ice Bear II," commissioned by John Stoneman, producer of the television program *The Last Frontier*, was featured in a show which aired in the Fall of 1990, and was now hanging in the Canadian Museum of Nature in Ottawa. Littlejohn, who was then 40 years of age, was a former K-Tel Records graphic artist, whose style had been compared to that of Bateman and Norman Rockwell. Born on Bell Island, he had hitchhiked to Ontario at the tender age of 14. That was 1964, several of the mines had already closed and he saw no future there. For a long time, he thought he would never return to Bell Island. In 1972, this self-taught artist was selling his ink drawings for $10.00 a piece. By 1990, the starting price for his small works was $3,500.00 and some works had sold for as high as $30,000.00. He came home to work on the Murals Project and direct the other artists, teaching them the techniques of high-realism. He devised a system of painting in which the artists worked in pairs to map out the murals on walls and then paint them. While one artist worked on a small-scale painting of the subject, another would create a grid on the wall, allowing a foot for each inch of the original painting. Littlejohn created "The Miner" (unveiled Nov. 9, 1991), "Miners' Monument" (unveiled New Year's Eve 1992), "On the Hub" (unveiled Dec. 29, 1995) and the "Steve Neary Memorial" (unveiled June 21, 1997).

There were seven other artists on the project:

Rick Murphy was a 22-year old who had just graduated from art school in Ontario when he learned about the Murals Project. He was born in Cambridge where his father, a Bell Islander, had moved to find work after the mines closed. Murphy assisted Littlejohn with "The Miner" and also worked on the "Miners' Monument," "On the Hub" and the "Steve Neary Memorial."

Bill Whalen grew up not far from No. 6 Mine. He was a teenager when the mines closed and his father tore down their house and moved the family to Spaniards Bay. Bill had worked for many years as a musician with the Newfoundland Showband before starting work on the murals. He was the only artist with any experience painting murals, having painted several on the walls of his friends' rec rooms as a hobby. Whalen supervised the younger artists during the summer of 1991. They painted small-scale scenes of Bell Island's history to determine which ones would be enlarged as murals. He then took over the painting of the "No. 6 Deck Head" mural on the C.L.B. Armoury after Jeff Parsons had completed the preliminary work, finishing it in late fall 1991. He also worked on the "On the Hub" mural and the "Steve Neary Memorial."

Jeff Parsons grew up in St. Philips where he had moved with his parents after the mines closed. He was an art student at Sheridan College in Ontario in 1991. He did the gridding and sketching of the "No. 6 Deck Head" mural and, at the end of the summer, returned to Ontario for his second year of studies.

Wayne Cole sketched the mural of "No. 3 Main Gate Area" on the former No. 3 Hoist House using photographs of the original mine site as his guide.

Gordon Johnson, for whom this project awakened an art interest that had lain dormant for 20 years, remembers playing in the area of No. 6 Mine, not far from where he grew up, and recalls being chased out of the mine a few times. He did the painting of "No. 3 Main Gate Area" when Wayne Cole had finished sketching it. It was unveiled on Christmas Eve 1991. Johnson also worked on the "Miners' Monument," the "On the Hub" mural and the "Steve Neary Memorial."

Richard Hawco and Scott Tremblett were school friends on Bell Island who had painted and drawn since grade 9. Together they painted the mural of "Town Square" on the Orange Lodge. It was finished in February 1992.

These eight artists painted in all weather conditions, wearing gloves when it was freezing cold. Some mornings, the first thing they would have to do was thaw the paint. They were assisted by a support crew of four, headed by Colin Cobb along with Aiden Fleming, Walt Vokey, and Francis Kennedy.

The fifth mural, the "Miners' Monument," differed in several ways from the first four. First of all, this mural is in three parts. The large central painting is of the Scotia Pocket, where the ore was deposited while awaiting shipment from Scotia Pier to steel mills around the world. The smaller painting to the left of it is entitled "Taking Five Underground" and shows a driller resting on his drill as he contemplates the job at hand. The model was Ray Stone. The smaller painting on the right is entitled "The Second Wash." It shows a miner at home washing his hands and face at an old-fashioned wash stand. The model was Don Decker. This mural was the first in which live models were used. It was also the first to be painted on a free-standing wall. The mural is associated with three separate plaques honouring Bell Island and its people. On a concrete platform in front of the paintings is the plaque erected by the Historic Sites and Monuments Board of Canada declaring the Wabana Iron Ore Mines a National Historic Site for being one of the world's premier iron ore mines and for its important contribution to the Newfoundland economy prior to Confederation with Canada. On the wall to either side of the mural are two plaques. The one on the left was commissioned by the Department of Tourism of Newfoundland honouring the Bell Island Mines on the 25th anniversary of Newfoundland's confederation with Canada. On the wall to the right of the mural is a memorial to those who lost their lives in mining-related accidents at Bell Island from 1895 to 1966. Littlejohn, Johnson and Murphy painted this mural during the summer and fall of 1992. It was unveiled on New Year's Eve of that year.

The sixth mural, entitled "On the Hub," was a massive undertaking. It was the first mural to be painted on a privately-owned building, Martin Hurley's warehouse on Theatre Avenue, the Green. The subject of the mural is a busy street scene, as Theatre Avenue looked in 1942 when it was still an important commercial district. This was the first mural to be populated by a large group of people, all live models. To prepare for this painting, the Murals Association advertised for people to model in 1940s-style clothing. On April 24th, 1993, a group of Bell Islanders and former Bell Islanders of all ages gathered on Theatre Avenue. There they spent several hours being photographed by Ron Bennett as they posed in period clothes that had been provided by Marie Sharpe, wardrobe mistress of the St. John's Arts and Culture Centre. Using these photographs and archival images of the street as his guide, Littlejohn then sketched out the mural and he and Gord Johnson proceeded with the painting. A shelter was constructed to protect the artists and the work-in-progress from the elements. Because of the fine detail involved, coupled with a shortage of funding, it took two and a half years to complete this mural. The two original artists were eventually joined by Bill Whalen and Rick Murphy. The mural was unveiled December 29th, 1995.

To commemorate Steve Neary, long-time MHA and advocate for Bell Island, a monument with an attached mural was unveiled in his honour on June 21, 1997. Steve had died a year earlier at the age of 70. This monument was first located at the Memorial Community Recreation Field on the west side of the former East Track (also called Railroad Street), which was renamed Steve Neary Boulevard in 1996. It was relocated next to the Royal Canadian Legion in 1998. The mural is a portrait of Steve Neary overlooking a scene depicting the eastern portion of Bell Island as seen from the Tickle. This mural was painted by Littlejohn, Johnson, Whalen and Murphy.

Several of the earlier murals have deteriorated due to exposure to the environment and problems with the process and materials that were used to create them. Two of these, the "Miners' Monument" and the "No. 6 Deck Head," were repainted by their original artists in the comfort of the former Trades School. When repainting the "Miners' Monument," John Littlejohn took the opportunity to enhance the central panel by superimposing over the image of Scotia Pier portraits of 17 former DOSCO employees: Bill Ford, William A. Newman, James Kavanagh, Gregory L. Gorman, William R. Power, John Cummings, Peter J. Kent, Alex McDonald, Alphonsus P. Hawco Jr., Elijah B. Blackmore, James J. Butler, Hector Cobb, James P. Delahunty, Dick Parsley, Charles O'Brien Sr., Lewis Pynn, and Thomas O'Keefe. This new rendering was installed over the old one in the summer of 2004. The original "No. 6 Deck Head" mural was removed from the CLB Armoury in 2002. The new version was installed on the west wall of the Fire Hall in the summer of 2005.

Sadly, the lead artist on the Murals Project, John Littlejohn, passed away on June 9, 2004 at the Kingston General Hospital Cancer Centre in Ontario. Following the completion of his masterpiece "On the Hub" mural, he and Rick Murphy had continued to work together, creating several aviation murals for the Town of Gander while training and supervising a group of young murals' artists there. Their work then took them to Cambridge, Ontario, where they formed a company and worked on a number of murals, the most notable of which is probably the huge three-piece mural done for the Galt Arena Gardens. The large centerpiece mural, entitled "The Fans," was composed in a similar fashion to the "On the Hub" mural. Prominent Cambridge sports figures posed for it, as did all the members of the Cambridge city council. Many of the faces in the crowd are former Bell Islanders. "The Fans" is flanked by portraits of hockey legend Gordie Howe and Detroit Red Wing Kirk Maltby. It was unveiled in 2002 with Gordie Howe in attendance. The work caught the attention of then Prime Minister, Jean Chretien, who invited the two artists to his office, where they presented him with a portrait of Gordie Howe. John, the son of a mining family, has left us with a fine legacy, both here in his home town and in his adopted Ontario home.

Photo by Henry Crane

Mural #1: "The Miner"

Subject:	William (Billy) Parsons, a miner for 51 years, is based on a Yousuf Karsh photograph taken shortly after Newfoundland joined Confederation. In the background is the plant of No. 3 Mine.
Location:	The east wall of the Wabana Complex (former Trades School / Community College)
Artists:	John Littlejohn and Rick Murphy
Size:	21' in diameter
Date:	Unveiled Nov. 9, 1991

Mural #2: "No. 6 Deck Head"

Subject: No. 6 Deck Head

Location: The Fire Hall west wall (was originally on the
             C.L.B. Armoury south wall)

Artists: Bill Whalen and Jeff Parsons

Size: 40' wide x 15.5' high

Date: Finished late fall 1991

Mural #3: "No. 3 Main Gate Area"

Subject: The buildings that made up No. 3 Mine plant, with the hoist house depicted in the far right panel.

Location: The east wall of the No. 3 hoist house

Artists: Gordon Johnson and Wayne Cole

Size: Approx. 42' wide x 13' high

Date: Unveiled Dec. 24, 1991

Photo by Gail Weir

Mural #4: "Town Square"

Subject: The lower end of Town Square from a picture
             taken in 1961. Front and centre in the mural is
             a 1927 Whippett driven by its owner Ned Kent.
             His passengers are his two daughters.

Location: The Loyal Orange Lodge north wall

Artists: Richard Hawco and Scott Tremblett

Size: Approx. 28' wide x 17' high

Date: Finished February 1992

Mural #5: "Miners' Monument"

Subject: The large central panel is of the Scotia Pocket superimposed with portraits of 17 former DOSCO employees. The smaller mural to the left of it, entitled "Taking Five Underground," shows a driller resting on his drill as he contemplates the job at hand. The smaller mural on the right, entitled "The Second Wash," shows a miner at home washing his hands and face at an old-fashioned wash stand.

On a concrete platform in front of the paintings is the plaque erected by the Historic Sites and Monuments Board of Canada declaring the Wabana Iron Ore Mines a National Historic Site. On the wall to either side of the mural are two plaques. The one on the left was commissioned by the Department of Tourism of Newfoundland honouring the Bell Island Mines on the 25th anniversary of Newfoundland's confederation with Canada. On the wall to the right of the mural is a memorial to those who lost their lives in mining-related accidents at Bell Island between 1895 to 1966.

Location: The small park east of the Post Office

Artists: John Littlejohn, Rick Murphy and Gordon Johnson

Size: 30' wide x 10' high

Date: Unveiled Dec. 31, 1992

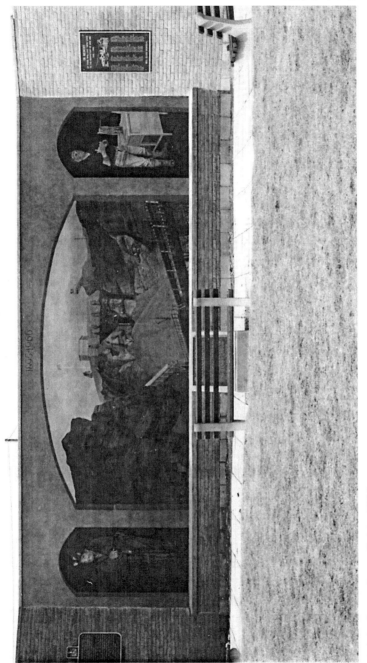

Original mural unveiled in 1992

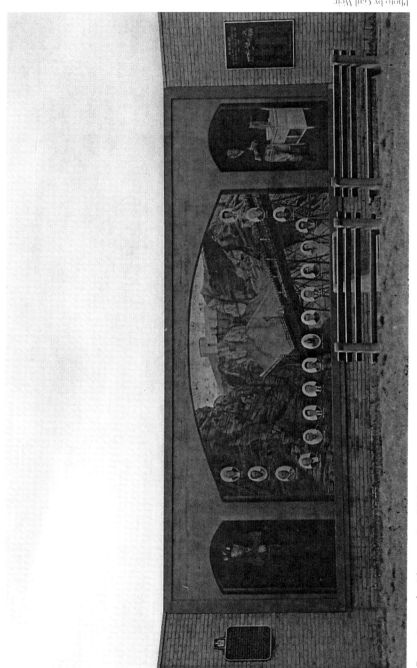

Present mural with portraits, 2005

188

189

Photo by Gail Weir

IN MEMORY
OF THOSE WHO GAVE THEIR LIVES
TO THE PRODUCTION OF IRON ORE
1895 – 1966

EDWARD POWER	JAMES WHALEN	JAMES BYRNE	JOHN BRAZIL
EDWARD KAVANAGH	THOMAS HAMCO	ALBERT WALSH	HECTOR COBB
WILLIAM CLAVINE	FRED TAYLOR	RICHARD LAHEY	THOMAS BUTLER
PAT FITZGERALD	JOHN BURSEY	JOHN LeGROW	ALBERT DROVER
WILLIAM BUGDEN	PAT McEVAY	SAMUEL PENNEY	HAYWARD GEORGE
CHARLES FITTON	WILLIAM SEWARD	HENRY SHEPPARD	MICHAEL KENNEDY
PETER DOYLE (AGE 14)	MICHAEL DINN	JAMES WHALEN	RANDALL SKANES
PAT CURRAN	PETER WADE	SAMUEL MURPHY	JAMES BUTLER
MICHAEL SMITH	PETER WINTERS	ROBERT YETMAN	SAM PEACH
CHARLES DAY	J.J. McKENZIE	WALTER DWYER	JOSEPH ANTHONY
HUBERT BRUCE	PAT HANLON	EDWARD DWYER	REGINALD DOBBIN
PETER BRAY	ELISHA SMITH	SYDNEY WARFORD	THOMAS BOYCE
EDWARD HALLORAN	AMBROSE CLARKE	SAMUEL COBB	JOHN CONNOLLY
EDWARD PENDERGAST	JOSIAH COOMBS	ANGUS MacDONALD	MICHAEL NUGENT
JAMES RYAN	STEWARD LUFFMAN	(ASST. MANAGER)	HAROLD DEAN
JOHN WALSH	THOMAS WALL	JAMES LEO FITZPATRICK	GERALD SHEA
MICHAEL BOLGER	JOHN ROSE	JOHN COSTELLO	WILLIAM ANTHONY
JORDAN DEERING	THOMAS GILL	FRANK COSTELLO	RICHARD BUTLER
BERNARD MORIARITY	WILLIAM HENNESSEY	THOMAS SWEENEY	ALPHONSUS HAMCO, JR.
RICHARD DELANEY	PETER FITZGERALD	JOHN W. GOSSE	ALBERT SLADE
CHARLES THOMAS	DENNIS POWER	EDMOND MERCER	JAMES KELLOWAY
JAMES MURPHY	EDWARD KING	WILLIAM LANE	GERALD COSTELLO
JOHN HUNT	PAT KELLY	MARTIN SHEPPARD	ERNEST YOKEY
GEORGE ANTLE	ED T. BARNES	SAMUEL CHAYTOR	WALTER C REES
JOHN KING	ISAAC CRANN	WILLIAM POWER	LEANDER GOSSE
PAT ABBOTT	GEORGE BISHOP	ROBERT DOMINEY	WILLIAM MILLER
			PATRICK KELLY

BELL ISLAND MEMORIAL

Plaque to the right of the mural

Photo by Gail Weir

THE WABANA MINES

The existence of iron ore on Bell Island was known as early as 1610 when Sir Percival Willoughby, whose family controlled extensive iron ore mines in England, petitioned that the Island be included in his grant so that he might exploit its potential.

Mining operations did not begin, however, until nearly three centuries later when the full extent of the ore deposits became known. In 1895, the first cargo of ore was shipped from here to Nova Scotia by the Nova Scotia Steel & Coal Company. The two independent companies initially involved in mining on Bell Island – the Nova Scotia Steel & Coal Company and the Dominion Iron & Steel Company – merged in 1921 to form the Dominion Steel Company which continued to manage the mines until their complete shutdown in 1966.

ERECTED TO COMMEMORATE THE 25TH ANNIVERSARY OF NEWFOUNDLAND'S CONFEDERATION WITH CANADA
DEPARTMENT OF TOURISM GOVERNMENT OF NEWFOUNDLAND AND LABRADOR.

Plaque to the left of the mural

THE WABANA IRON ORE MINES
LES MINES DE FER DE WABANA

Although the presence of iron ore on Bell Island was known as early as the 16th century, it was not until 1895 that the Nova Scotia Coal and Steel Company opened the first mine. The link with Nova Scotia lasted through a succession of corporate owners until the mines' closure in 1966. These mines, reaching some five kilometres under Conception Bay, were for many years among the world's major sources of iron ore. Their development gave Newfoundland a measure of prosperity prior to World War I, and they remained a mainstay of the country's economy for four decades.

On connaissait la présence de minerai de fer dans l'île Bell dès le XVIe siècle, mais la Nova Scotia Coal and Steel Company n'y ouvrit une première mine qu'en 1895. Le lien avec la Nouvelle-Écosse dura, malgré plusieurs changements de propriétaires, jusqu'à la fermeture des mines, en 1966. Celles-ci, qui s'étendaient jusqu'à cinq kilomètres sous la baie Conception, furent longtemps parmi les principales sources de fer du monde. Leur exploitation assura une certaine prospérité à Terre-Neuve avant la Première Guerre mondiale, et elles demeurèrent l'un des pivots de l'économie du pays pendant les quatre décennies suivantes.

Historic Sites and Monuments Board of Canada.
Commission des lieux et monuments historiques du Canada.

Government of Canada - Gouvernement du Canada

Plaque in front of the mural

Photo by Gail Weir

Mural #6: "On the Hub"

Subject: Theatre Avenue on the Green in 1942 showing the Gaiety Theatre and St. Peter's Roman Catholic Church and surrounding shops and buildings. The mural is populated by more than 200 people in a busy Christmas scene.

Location: The west wall of Martin Hurley's warehouse on Theatre Avenue, the Green

Artists: John Littlejohn and Gordon Johnson, with Bill Whalen and Rick Murphy

Size: 50' wide x 8' high

Date: Unveiled Dec. 29, 1995

Mural #7: "Steve Neary Memorial Monument"

Subject:	Portrait of Steve Neary with the eastern portion of Bell Island as seen from the Tickle
Location:	The parking lot of the Royal Canadian Legion
Artists:	John Littlejohn, Gordon Johnson, Bill Whalen and Rick Murphy
Size:	7' in diameter
Date:	Unveiled June 21, 1997

WORKS CITED

Anson, C.M. "The Wabana Iron Ore Properties of the Dominion Steel and Coal Corporation, Limited." *Canadian Mining and Metallurgical Bulletin* 473 (1951): 597-602.

Anspach, Lewis A. *A History of the Island of Newfoundland.* London: Sherwood, Gilbert, and Piper, 1827.

Baker, Melvin. "Prominent Figures from our Recent Past: Edward M. Jackman." *Newfoundland Quarterly* 87.3 (1992): 36-37.

Bown, Addison. "Newspaper History of Bell Island." [Queen Elizabeth II Library, Memorial University of Newfoundland.]

-------. "The Ore-Boat Sinkings at Bell Island in 1942." Address. Rotary Club. St. John's, Newfoundland, 15 Nov. 1962. [Newfoundland Section, A.C. Hunter Provincial Reference Library.]

"Butler Family Papers." P6/B/62. Provincial Archives of Newfoundland and Labrador.

Cantley, Thomas. "The Wabana Iron Mines of the Nova Scotia Steel and Coal Company Limited." *Canadian Mining Institute Journal* 14 (1911): 274-99.

Caplan, Ronald. *Views From the Steel Plant: Voices and Photographs from 100 Years of Making Steel in Cape Breton Island.* Wreck Cove: Breton Books, 2005.

Cell, Gillian T. *English Enterprise in Newfoundland, 1577-1660.* Toronto: University of Toronto Press, 1969.

Census of Newfoundland and Labrador 1901. St. John's: His Majesty's Printing Office, 1903.

Chambers, R.E., and A.R. Chambers. "The Sinking of the Wabana Submarine Slopes." *Canadian Mining Institute Journal* 12 (1909): 139-48.

Courage, John R. "A Capsule History of the National Convention." *The Book of Newfoundland*. Ed. Joseph R. Smallwood. 6 vols. St. John's: Newfoundland Book Publishers (1967) Ltd., 1975. 5: 169-181.

Cuff, Robert C. "Jackman, David Ignatius," and "Jackman, David Joseph." *Encyclopedia of Newfoundland and Labrador*. Gen. ed. Joseph R. Smallwood. 5 vols. St. John's: Newfoundland Book Publishers (1967) Limited, 1981-1994. 3: 88.

Day, E.E., and R.E. Pearson. "Closure of the Bell Island Iron Ore Mines." *Geography* 52 (1967): 320-25.

"Disaster Hits Bell Island." *The Evening Telegram* [St. John's, NL], 21 Apr. 1966: 6.

"Dwindling Ore Markets Shatter Economic Life of Bell Island." *The Evening Telegram* [St. John's, NL], 20 Apr. 1966: 1.

Elver, R.B. *The Canadian Iron Ore Industry in 1962*. Mineral Information Bulletin MR 67. Ottawa: Department of Mines and Technical Surveys, 1963.

Fay, C.R. *Life and Labour in Newfoundland*. Cambridge: W. Heffer and Sons, 1956.

Green, J. Derek. "Miners' Unions on Bell Island." Unpublished B. Comm. paper. Memorial University of Newfoundland, 1968.

Hadley, Michael L. *U-Boats Against Canada: German Submarines in Canadian Waters*. Montreal: McGill-Queen's University Press, 1985.

Hakluyt, Richard. *The Principal Navigations, Voyages, Traffiques and Discoveries of the English Nation*. 12 vols. Glasgow: James Maclehose and Sons, 1904. Vol. 8.

Hanington, Dan. "Twice Torpedoed, He Joined the Navy!" Trident 18.21 (1984): 1, 12, 13.

Hattenhauer, Rolfe G. Coll-079. Rolfe G. Hattenhauer Papers. Archives and Manuscripts Division, Queen Elizabeth II Library, Memorial University of Newfoundland.

Hayes, Albert O. *Wabana Iron Ore of Newfoundland*. Geological Survey Memoir 78, No. 66. Ottawa: Government Printing Bureau, 1915.

Hodge, Frederick Webb, ed. *Handbook of American Indians North of Mexico*. Smithsonian Institution Bureau of American Ethnology Bulletin 30. New York: Greenwood Press, 1969.

Janes, T.H., and R.B. Elver. *Survey of the Canadian Iron Ore Industry During 1958*. Mineral Information Bulletin MR 31. Ottawa: Department of Mines and Technical Surveys, 1959.

-------. *A Survey of the Iron Ore Industry in Canada During 1957*. Mineral Information Bulletin MR 27. Ottawa: Department of Mines and Technical Surveys, 1958.

Labour Gazette 49 (1949): 1329; 50 (1950): 422, 1126; 51 (1951): 1444.

"Marine Court Inquiry into Bell Island Disaster 1940." GN 2/5:787. Provincial Archives of Newfoundland and Labrador.

Martin, Wendy. *Once Upon a Mine: Story of Pre-Confederation Mines on the Island of Newfoundland*. Montreal: Canadian Institute of Mining and Metallurgy, 1983.

McAllister, R.I. *The Structure of the Newfoundland Population*. St. John's: Government of Newfoundland, 1965.

Narváez, Peter. "The Protest Songs of a Labor Union on Strike Against an American Corporation in a Newfoundland Company Town; A Folkloristic Analysis with Special References to Oral Folk History." Diss. Indiana University, 1986.

Neary, Peter. "'Traditional' and 'Modern' Elements in the Social and Economic History of Bell Island and Conception Bay." *Canadian Historical Association Historical Papers* (1973): 105-136.

Schneider, V.B. *Canadian Iron Ore Industry 1966*. Mineral Information Bulletin MR 89. Ottawa: Department of Energy, Mines and Resources, 1968.

Seary, E.R. *Place Names of the Avalon Peninsula of the Island of Newfoundland*. Toronto: University of Toronto Press, 1971.

Smallwood, Joseph R. "Newfoundland's Island of Iron." *The Evening Telegram* [St. John's, NL] 24 Apr. 1920: 4; 27 Apr. 1920: 11.

Southey, V.J. "History and Problems of the Wabana Submarine Iron Mines." *C.I.M. Bulletin* 62 (1969): 371-96.

Submarine Miner 1.2 (1954): n.p.

"Tabloid History of Coal and Steel Industry in Nova Scotia." *Financial Post*, 2 July 1926: 16.

"Union Leader Leaves to Reside in Montreal." *The Evening Telegram* [St. John's, NL], 9 Oct. 1964: 5.

Wabana. Dir. Joe Harvey. Prod. Extension Services, Memorial University of Newfoundland, 1974.

Wells, Herb. *Under the White Ensign.* 1 vol. to date. St. John's: By the author, 1977- . Vol. 1.

Wittur, G.E. *Canadian Iron Ore Industry 1963*. Mineral Information Bulletin MR 76. Ottawa: Department of Mines and Technical Surveys, 1964.

-------. *Canadian Iron Ore Industry 1964*. Mineral Information Bulletin MR 80. Ottawa: Department of Mines and Technical Surveys, 1965.

ENDNOTES

1   Lewis Amadeus Anspach, *A History of the Island of Newfoundland* (London: By the author, 1819), 301.

2   Anspach, 368.

3   Richard Hakluyt, *The Principal Navigations Voyages Traffiques & Discoveries of the English Nation*, 12 vols. (Glasgow: MacLehose, 1904), 8: 15.

4   Gillian T. Cell, *English Enterprise in Newfoundland, 1577-1660* (Toronto: University of Toronto Press, 1969), 72.

5   "Butler Family Papers," P6/B/62, Provincial Archives of Newfoundland and Labrador. [Papers and documents pertaining to the original leases on the mining property on Bell Island.]

6   C.R. Fay, *Life and Labour in Newfoundland* (Cambridge: Hefer, 1956), 217-18.

7   R.E. Chambers and A.R. Chambers, "The Sinking of the Wabana Submarine Slopes," *Canadian Mining Institute Journal* 12 (1909): 139.

8   Thomas Cantley, "The Wabana Iron Mines of the Nova Scotia Steel and Coal Company Limited," *Canadian Mining Institute Journal* 14 (1911): 274; E.R. Seary, *Place Names of the Avalon Peninsula of the Island of Newfoundland* (Toronto: U of Toronto P, 1971), 26; and Frederick Webb Hodge, *Handbook of American Indians North of Mexico*, Smithsonian Institution Bureau of American Ethnology Bulletin 30 (New York: Greenwood, 1969), 2-6, who states that the name *Abnaki*, used by Algonquian tribes living in the state of Maine and along the Atlantic seaboard, is from *Wabunaki*, meaning "eastland" or "morning land."

9   Addison Bown, "Newspaper History of Bell Island," 1: 3. [Mr. Bown gleaned all references to Bell Island between the years 1894 and 1939 from the pages of *The Daily News*. His compilation of these news items is bound into two volumes which are held at the Queen Elizabeth II Library, Memorial University of Newfoundland.]

10 Cantley, 276-77.

11 Cantley, 274.

12 Bown, "Newspaper," 1: 4, 7.

13 Ronald Caplan, *Views From the Steel Plant: Voices and Photographs from 100 Years of Making Steel in Cape Breton Island* (Wreck Cove: Breton Books, 2005), 213.

14 Bown, "Newspaper," 1: 8.

15 Chambers, 139.

16 C.M. Anson, "The Wabana Iron Ore Properties of the Dominion Steel and Coal Corporation, Limited," *Canadian Mining and Metallurgical Bulletin* 473 (1951): 601; and Caplan, 213.

17 Albert Orion Hayes, *Wabana Iron Ore of Newfoundland*, Geological Survey Memoir 78, No. 66 (Ottawa: Government Printing Bureau, 1915), 5.

18 Cantley, 275.

19 Joseph R. Smallwood, "Newfoundland's Island of Iron," *The Evening Telegram* [St. John's, NL], 24 Apr. 1920: 4; 27 Apr. 1920: 11.

20 Anson, 599.

21 "Tabloid History of Coal and Steel Industry in Nova Scotia," *Financial Post*, 2 July 1926: 16; and Caplan, 214.

22 Wendy Martin, *Once Upon A Mine* (Montreal: Canadian Institute of Mining and Metallurgy, 1983), 52-54; and Caplan, 214.

23 *Census of Newfoundland and Labrador 1901* (St. John's: HMPO, 1903), xxvii, 2, 6; and Bown, "Newspaper," 1: 18.

24 Cantley, 283; and Bown, "Newspaper," 1: 11, 19, 20.

[25] E.E. Day and R.E. Pearson, "Closure of the Bell Island Iron Ore Mines," *Geography* 52 (1967): 324.

[26] R.I. McAllister, *The Structure of the Newfoundland Population* (St. John's: Government of Newfoundland, 1965), 10.

[27] Anson, 601.

[28] T.H. Janes and R.B. Elver, *A Survey of the Iron Ore Industry in Canada During 1957*, Mineral Information Bulletin MR 27 (Ottawa: Department of Mines and Technical Surveys, 1958), 15.

[29] T.H. Janes and R.B. Elver, *Survey of the Canadian Iron Ore Industry During 1958*, Mineral Information Bulletin MR 31 (Ottawa: Department of Mines and Technical Surveys, 1959), 56.

[30] R.B. Elver, *The Canadian Iron Ore Industry in 1962*, Mineral Information Bulletin MR 67 (Ottawa: Department of Mines and Technical Surveys, 1963), 47-48; and "Disaster Hits Bell Island," *The Evening Telegram* [St. John's, NL], 21 Apr. 1966: 6.

[31] Day, 323-24.

[32] G.E. Wittur, *Canadian Iron Ore Industry 1963*, Mineral Information Bulletin MR 76 (Ottawa: Department of Mines and Technical Surveys, 1964), 50; and "Dwindling Ore Markets Shatter Economic Life of Bell Island," *The Evening Telegram* [St. John's, NL], 20 Apr. 1966: 1.

[33] G.E. Wittur, *Canadian Iron Ore Industry 1964*, Mineral Information Bulletin MR 80 (Ottawa: Department of Mines and Technical Surveys, 1965), 65.

[34] V.B. Schneider, *Canadian Iron Ore Industry 1966*, Mineral Information Bulletin MR 89 (Ottawa: Department of Energy, Mines and Resources, 1968), 1.

[35] Day, 322; and V.J. Southey, "History and Problems of the Wabana Submarine Iron Mines," *C.I.M. Bulletin* 62 (1969): 382.

[36] Bown, "Newspaper" 1: 5.

[37] Bown, "Newspaper" 1: 10.

[38] Bown, "Newspaper" 1: 12-13; Melvin Baker, "Prominent Figures from our Recent Past: Edward M. Jackman," *Newfoundland Quarterly* 87.3 (1992): 36; and J. Derek Green, "Miners' Unions on Bell Island," unpublished B. Comm. paper, Memorial University of Newfoundland, 1968, 13.

[39] Bown, "Newspaper" 1: 19, 24.

[40] Bown, "Newspaper" 2: 1-2; Rolfe G. Hattenhauer Collection, Archives and Manuscripts Division, Queen Elizabeth II Library, Memorial University of Newfoundland, COLL-079: 68.01.001; and Green, 31.

[41] Bown, "Newspaper" 1: 72, 2: 7-8. For a discussion of the difficulty the Newfoundland fisherman-turned-miner had accepting the schedules and "living by the clock" required of industrial life, see Peter Narváez, "The Protest Songs of a Labor Union on Strike Against an American Corporation in a Newfoundland Company Town," diss., Indiana U, 1986, 64-67; and Peter Neary, "'Traditional' and 'Modern' Elements in the Social and Economic History of Bell Island and Conception Bay," *Canadian Historical Association Historical Papers* (1973): 130.

[42] Green, 34.

[43] Bown, "Newspaper" 2: 23.

[44] Hattenhauer, 68.02.003; and Green, 51.

[45] Robert H. Cuff, "Jackman, David Ignatius," and "Jackman, David Joseph," Joseph R. Smallwood, gen. ed., *Encyclopedia of Newfoundland and Labrador*, 5 vols. (St. John's: Newfoundland Book Publishers (1967) Limited, 1991) vol. 3: 88.

[46] Baker, 36.

[47] Green, 48.

[48] Green, 49, 52.

[49] Hattenhauer, 68.02.002: 21.

[50] Hattenhauer, 68.02.002: 33.

[51] Hattenhauer, 68.02.001: 31-32.

[52] Green, 67, 68, 71, 75; and *Labour Gazette* 49 (1949): 1329; 50 (1950): 422, 1126; 51 (1951): 1444.

[53] John R. Courage, "A Capsule History of the National Convention," Joseph R. Smallwood, ed., *The Book of Newfoundland*, 6 vols. (St. John's: Newfoundland Book Publishers (1967) Ltd., 1975) 5: 171.

[54] Cuff, "Jackman, David Ignatius," 3: 88.

[55] Joseph R. Smallwood was the Liberal Premier of Newfoundland from 1949, when Newfoundland entered Confederation with Canada, until 1972.

[56] "Union Leader Leaves to Reside in Montreal," *The Evening Telegram* [St. John's, NL] 9 Oct. 1964: 5; and Green, 83-86, 96-97.

[57] "Marine Court Inquiry into Bell Island Disaster 1940," GN 2/5:787, Provincial Archives of Newfoundland and Labrador.

[58] MUNFLA, Ms., 78-175/pp. 20-21.

[59] MUNFLA, Ms., 75-226/p. 2.

[60] Herb Wells, *Under the White Ensign*, 1 vol. to date (St. John's: By the author, 1977-) 1: 42-45; and Michael L. Hadley, *U-Boats Against Canada* (Montreal: McGill-Queen's UP, 1985), 114, 116, 142, 149, 152.

[61] Addison Bown, "The Ore-Boat Sinkings At Bell Island in 1942," address, Rotary Club of St. John's, 15 Nov. 1962. Dan Hanington, a survivor of the *PLM 27*, gives a first-person account of the events surrounding the two attacks, the sinking of his ship, his attempt to save a shipmate, and being rescued on Lance Cove Beach in *Trident* 18.21 (1984): 12-13.

[62] MUNFLA, Tape, 84-119/C7621.

[63] MUNFLA, Ms., 70-20/p. 61.

[64] Hadley, 142, states that she was hit on Oct. 20, sixteen miles southeast of Ferryland Head and, after a twenty-minute delay, continued on with the journey.

[65] MUNFLA, Ms., 75-226/pp. 2-3.

[66] MUNFLA, Ms., 79-88/p. 8.

[67] MUNFLA, Survey Card, 71-22/43.

[68] Bown, "Newspaper" 1: 11, 19, 28, 32.

[69] *Submarine Miner*, 1.2 (1954): n. pag., states that the company whistle, known locally as the "bull-dog," was installed at No. 2 Sub Station on Mar. 24th, 1924. It was later moved to No. 3 Main Hoist. It blew automatically to signal the changing of the shifts and the mid-day meal hour. When there was a house fire, the telephone operators at the Avalon Telephone Company activated a switch which caused the whistle to blow a certain number of times, depending on which section of the Island the fire was located. Man trams, also called man rakes, were tram cars fitted with seats. Each car could carry thirty-two men.

[70] MUNFLA, Ms., 78-189/p. 2.

[71] MUNFLA, Survey Card, 70-20/91.

[72] MUNFLA, Ms., 70-20/p. 6; MUNFLA, Tape, 78-189/C4522.

[73] MUNFLA, Tape, 84-119/C7621.

[74] MUNFLA, Ms., 74-44/p. 21.

[75] H.P. Dickey was Vice-President and General Manager of Dominion Wabana Ore Limited in the early 1950s.

[76] MUNFLA, Ms., 71-109/p. 37.

[77] Bown, "Newspaper" 1: 40.

[78] MUNFLA, Ms., 71-109/p. 47.

[79] MUNFLA, Ms., 79-87/p. 4.

[80] MUNFLA, Survey Card, 70-20/98.

[81] MUNFLA, Ms., 71-109/p. 46.

[82] MUNFLA, Ms., 78-175/p. 26.

[83] MUNFLA, Ms., 78-175/pp. 24-25.

[84] MUNFLA, Ms., 75-230/p. 13.

[85] MUNFLA, Tape, 80-15/C5547.

[86] MUNFLA, Ms., 73-171/p. 19.

[87] MUNFLA, Ms., 75-230/p. 13.

[88] MUNFLA, Tape, 84-119/C7621.

[89] MUNFLA, Survey Card, 70-20/57; MUNFLA, Ms., 71-109/p. 38; MUNFLA, Ms., 72-97/p. 13; MUNFLA, Ms., 73-171/p. 24; MUNFLA, Ms., 74-74/p. 6; MUNFLA, Ms., 75-230/p. 12; and MUNFLA, Ms., 79-88/p. 7.

[90] MUNFLA, Tape, 72-95/C1278.

[91] MUNFLA, Ms., 72-97/p.13; MUNFLA, Ms., 74-74/p.6; and MUNFLA, Ms., 75-230/pp.12-13.

[92] MUNFLA, Ms., 72-97/p. 13; and MUNFLA, Ms., 74-74/p. 6.

[93] MUNFLA, Tape, 72-97/C1284.

[94] MUNFLA, Ms., 72-95/pp. 48-49.

[95] MUNFLA, Ms., 73-171/pp. 13-14.

[96] MUNFLA, Tape, 72-97/C1284.

[97] MUNFLA, Ms., 73-171/p. 19.

[98] MUNFLA, Ms., 71-75/pp. 21-23.

[99] MUNFLA, Ms., 81-055/pp. 3-6.

[100] *Wabana*, dir. Joe Harvey, prod. Extension Services, Memorial University of Newfoundland, 1974.

[101] MUNFLA, Survey Card, 70-20/73.

CPSIA information can be obtained
at www.ICGtesting.com
Printed in the USA
LVOW11s2236190917
549337LV00001B/1/P